Ploop!
The Abundant Pregnancy Journey

Omileye Achikeobi – Lewis

Omileye Achikeobi-Lewis

Naked Truth Book
UK, United States
A Naked Truth Book
P. O. Box 461
South Carolina, SC 29720

www.yeyeosun.com

DEDICATION

To all the women who want to be lifted to the sky. To all our Mothers, Grandmothers and Grandmother's Grandmothers who showed us how.

Note to the Reader

.

CONTENTS

ACKNOWLEDGMENTS

I give much thanks to my family: Derrick (my husband), Omololu and Kem Ra (my two children) – for all their support and willingness to eat so many TV dinners so that I could get this done!; my mother and brother for their constant support. I also give much thanks to the all above and all those who came before me, and on the shoulder of whose wisdom I stand.

.

INTRODUCTION

DANCING THE PATH

When I had Kem Ra I was determined to have a natural pregnancy. I was 25 and everyone advised me against it. But I just knew I had to dance the path of pregnancy in my own way. Against all the good advice I found a beautiful Natural Birthing Midwife, and joined other women in dancing and weaving our own paths to pregnancy. I still had all the tut tut tuts from my then partner's family and others who fed me many horror stories about all the things that would go wrong. But my homebirth midwife assured me of all the things that could and would go right. They helped me to breathe, and trust my body instinct. I thanked them for helping me to truly embrace the beauty of my personal journey.

During my pregnancy journey with Kem Ra I was a great lover of yoga and meditation, so I yogered and meditated my way all the way through the pregnancy. There was an ancient Egyptian mantra that I loved. It belonged to the Goddess of Birthing, and was so soothing. I used that mantra when I was giving birth to Kem Ra. I remember how mom sat in the hospital room, with her head wrapped, and quietly chanted it as I gave birth.

No you didn't misread. I did up end up in Hospital for the last two hours of my six hour labor which began at home. My lovely midwives had found myconian (baby poop) in my waters and gave me the choice of going to hospital. There was the possibility the baby was in distress. Although, I did the responsible thing and went to hospital I knew the baby was okay. I had been to my Jamaican cousin's birthday party the night before and knew that all the whining I did was the result of the poop in the water.

When I got to hospital I felt blessed. I had a homebirth setting where my midwives were fully present. Although I had only been four hours in labor the doctors were adamant that if I went anywhere beyond another hour in labor they were going to give me a caesarian. That was a little stressful, but my faithful beautiful midwives were not having it. They stood by my side, and ensured I had the beautiful birthing experience I deserved and had planned.

Kem Ra came out around 6.30 pm and flew right into the hands of his father. As I was being coaxed all the time through the push process the tear damage was minimal. I held Kem Ra triumphantly in my arms and smiled, I had the birthing experience I had always desired. There were no pain killers, no stirrups, not too much stress, mantras floating in the background, my mother present, his father present, beautiful smells in the air, and a memory worth holding onto. All those who had doubted I could dance my pregnancy safely my own natural way were truly surprised that all went well.

Dancing the Second Time Round

If I was 25 when I was pregnant with Kem Ra. I was 40 when I was pregnant with Omololu. It was 2009, and I was no longer living in the United Kingdom I was living in the United States. Here women did not seem encouraged to have natural births. Plus, where my natural birth in the UK was covered by the government as part of our National Health Care system, in the US I had the natural option but only if I could pay. That was okay, but we did not have the finances to do that at the time. My only option at that particular time seemed to be to have a hospital birth.

There also seemed to be a tendency to give women more medication here than in the UK, but I was adamant that I wanted as natural a birth as possible. My pregnancy with Omo tested everything I had from the beginning. I was forced to put all my natural know how (much of which I drew from my Ayurvedic and Island background) into practice.

Actually I had to put that know how into practice long before I had Omo. For when myself and Derrick decided to have a baby I had one big challenge ahead of me – the hurdle of remedying a 15 year period of infertility (I will share with you how I did that soon).

With Omo my pregnancy felt much harder on my body. Even though I look younger than my years, my body told me I was definitely all of 40 years old. I was more tired, and achier during this second dance of pregnancy. As a result, I had to try even harder than I remembered with Kem Ra to have the experience that I truly desired.

However, it was also during this second pregnancy dance that I had a deep transformational experience. I became extremely conscious of my inner power and wisdom. I can't explain it, but I felt that the wisdom and power within was fully present and teaching me about me, life and the baby. I felt that if I listened to it very carefully I would be guided in the right way.

It was during this period that I came up with a whole product line for mommies and babies. For every ailment I had I created a remedy for it. I stirred, and blended products I constantly had it at the forefront of my mind that we can all have beautiful pregnancy experiences. There was a strong feeling that as we women claimed back our pregnancy dances – we claimed back our lives.

The stirrup came to be a big symbol that dominated my mind. It represented bondage to me. I didn't know how it was going to happen, but I knew that I didn't want my legs to be up in the stirrups when I had Omo. Judging from my OBGYN's face when I said I would like to give birth on all fours, I thought, "Oh well, stirrups I will be forced into". This was a true point of stress for me. Derrick constantly assured me everything was going to be all right.

The Dance of Writing This Book

Writing this book has an interesting history and motivation. Straight after giving birth to Omo, I felt that I owed it to the sisterhood of pregnant mothers to record my experiences, the remedies and tools I used for a natural birthing experience. I think I also wrote this book because so many people were astounded that I gave birth naturally at home with no medication, remedied my fertility in forty days and had a completely natural pregnancy, and a natural at home 45 minute birthing experience (Omo plooped right on out and was delivered by Derrick, her dad). These people wanted to know more so I felt a further duty to share my experiences.

In writing this book, deep down I wanted more women to realize that their body has it. That we have generations of natural birthing memory right there in our DNA. I think I also wanted more women to simply have truly joyful and beautiful natural birthing experiences. Ones that left them with an experience of fullness and not emptiness, happiness and not pain, a warm heart and not a heart filled with regrets.

I also wanted women to realize there were natural remedies and mind-body energy tools that could help them to have wonderful, manageable, and accelerated healing processes in terms of their Dance of Fertility, Dance of Pregnancy, and Dance of Post Pregnancy experiences. Throughout this book, I have detailed the Seven Principles of Wellness I always teach to others. These principles are based on fundamental healing principles of Ayurvedic, world healing practices, and years of my life healing experiences. The Seven Principles of Wellness (detailed fully in the first segment of this book: Dance of Pregnancy) should be referred to often as you embrace your own abundant pregnancy journey. These principles help you to increase overall mind-body and soul nourishment.

With this motivation in mind I began what was quite a crazy journey of writing mostly with the computer upside down (so excuse any grammatical errors or typos), and with my foot firmly stuck on the baby bouncer. The main bulk of this book was finished by the time Omo was about three months old. However,

Omo is now almost two years and I am just about ready to Ploop! it on out. However just before "Plcop!" Plooped! It appeared to be waiting for something to happen before it do so. I was not sure what. Derrick, my husband and one of the heroes in this story, suggested "just wait. Ploop! is not ready to Ploop!"

Being the impatient soul that I am, I unwillingly but knowingly accepted this to be true. I had written a fair few books in my days to know when a book was ready to birth itself, or not.

Then two things happened just recently that helped me to understand why Ploop! was not Plooping!: One was the meeting of a beautiful Navajo Sister, Beth Robertson. Beth is a Master Weaver (my words not hers. She is way to humble to call herself a Master Weaver, but she really is) who helps people to weave the healing right into their lives. She is also an experienced Doula.

Myself and Beth spent many hours talking about the dance of birthing and the empowering messages it carries for us women in every stage of our lives. We both believed that when a woman claims her birthing journey she claims back something very raw, primordial and important. She somehow claims back her power and a future for the generations ahead. A future where we all begin to believe in our innate primordial power.

Beth shared that in her Navajo culture the birthing journey is called Hozho "Walking in Beauty". I thought that was a beautiful and fitting concept. For I sincerely believed during the dance of my second pregnancy with Omo that all women should feel beautiful during every stage of the birthing journey (which includes the after experience).

The more myself and Beth spoke, was the more we both believed that there was an inextricable force pulling us and other women together to bring the power, beauty and grace of the birthing experience into every stage of a woman and in fact the whole family's life. Right now we are in the middle of putting the threads of these dreams together and hopefully by the grace of the dancing angels around us we will share the ancient wisdom of birthing in workshops together, and with others who share the beauty of this vision.

Now a second thing happened just recently that completely hurtled "Ploop!" out. It was the encountering of the beautiful art work of Lori Portka. I first spied her artwork in the May 2012 issue of Natural Awakening Charlotte SC. I felt so drawn to it that I went to her website, fell in love with her artwork even more. It seemed to sing and dance with the energy and sweet whispers of the threads of life that weaves itself into all of our existences. I then went on to do something quite unusual. I called Lori and explained to her how much I loved her artwork. She was very sweet on the phone. I explained to her that I saw a vision of her artwork on the cover of one of my books. When I spoke to her I didn't think that book was going to be "Ploop!". Latter that evening after coming of the phone to her, I realized it was "Ploop!" for I saw a picture she did called "Lift Her Up to the Sky!". It was a picture of a pregnant woman in a yoga pose. That was it. I kept on looking at the picture and the picture kept on resonating with me. It seemed to sum up what "Ploop! The Abundant Pregnancy Journey" was really all about. It was all about us all feeling thoroughly empowered and lifted up to the sky.

So on that note, and with no further a due it is my sincere prayer that that we all feel "Lifted up to the Sky" and discover the sure steps of our own dance in this journey of life which consist of many birthing stages beginning with the Dance of Pregnancy. May we all remember too that the birthing process is no ordinary thing, but a timeless ritual of a cosmological process that is repeated in every aspect and layer of nature. This ritual reminds us that all of life is sacred, starting with the child we carry within.

Be blessed and abundant

Omileye, 2012

PART ONE

THE DANCE OF FERTILITY: SPERM SAY HELLO TO EGG

A Shinto Impregnation

I understand that the journey to fertility doesn't feel so much like a dance for most women. It is a journey that can be stressed ladened, because of how it is often approached by the medical field, and then there are the pressures couples put on themselves.

All the way back in 2007 ABC had a story about stress and infertility. They reported how a Dr. Sarah Berga, of Emory University School of Medicine had studied the impact of stress on fertility for years, said while humans are designed to deal with a certain amount of stress, chronic stress may prevent some women from ovulating. She said it starts with the hypothalamus, the part of the brain that controls the release of hormones.

"Your brain is hard to fool. If you're under eating, overworking and over exercising, the hypothalamus is, in essence, keeping a running tally of what you're doing," Berga said. "Even though you can say to yourself, 'I'm not stressed.' Your hypothalamus may come up with a different answer."

Apparently If the hypothalamus senses stress, the messages sent to the ovary to release eggs may be interrupted and cause stress-induced infertility.

I believe that the fertility journey can become a dance. A very joyous one, where we begin to tune into our own bodies and its tremendous power for self healing. I believe that during the fertility journey we can have fun, and love ourselves all the way through the process. It can be a great opportunity to pamper and restore your mind, body and soul. It can be chance to learn to love ourselves and relationships again. "What is she talking about?" I can hear you saying, but I am going to repeat it quite boldly – fertility can be a dance of joy.

The fertility journey does not have to be a long drawn out affair either. I believe it can be an accelerated process done through restoring balance the natural way. This is the gift that I believe Ayurveda, which means the Science of Life, has given to me – knowing the swift ancient secrets to restoring and replenishing the mind – body and soul. I hold my own forty day fertility cure up as proof. Once myself and Derrick decided to try for a child, I put all that I knew into action. Within forty days I had remedied fifteen years of infertility.

The process was not stressful to me, it was enjoyable. We both viewed the process with wide open hearts, eyes and wonderment.

It could be how the whole journey started of in the first place. One day I was browsing amongst the books of our local library when I came across an interesting little book about the Japanese religion Shintoism. The book attracted me, like all things that have a mystical element to it. I also knew that the Shinto tradition has a great reverence of nature, so that also attracted me to the book. As I flicked quickly through its pages I happened upon a chapter which talked about a popular Shinto method of praying. One that healed all forms of sickness. The author swore by this prayer method of writing your request on a piece of paper, leaving it in a sacred place for a specific number of days and then burning it. The fire was said to help transmute the problem from something negative to something positive. I was fascinated.

When I got home I casually shared my findings with Derrick. He listened quietly and then out of the blue he said,

"Let's pray for a baby,"

I laughed so hard I could not stop laughing.

"You think that Shinto prayer thing is going to help us to have a baby?" I asked.

"We could try it."

I looked into his eyes and knew he was as serious as serious could be. He really wanted to Shinto a baby in.

"What do we have to do?" he asked.

"Well, you have to write your prayer on a piece of paper; leave it in a special place for a certain number of days; then burn it after that number of days."

"Why burn it?" he asked.

"Because, they say that smoke carries things up to the heavens," I replied.

"Okay, let's set the prayer for forty days, and be celibate," Derrick suggested.

My eyes widened, "Celibate. You celibate for forty days?" I teased.

"Yes," he said seriously. "I think during that period you should put all your wellness stuff to the test."

"Are you up for the challenge?" he asked.

"Sure," I said, not truly believing he could be celibate for forty days.

Well, Derrick surprised me he really did stick to those forty days of celibacy. During that period I did all the things I knew that brought body, mind and spirit balance: massage, meditations, healthy eating etc etc etc.

After the forty days we broke our celibacy. In the few months that followed I felt achy and fluey all the time. I swore to Derrick I was going through the menopause. He kept on telling me I was pregnant, but I was still having periods so I sincerely doubted it.

Eventually I succumbed and went to The Dollar store to get a cheap pregnancy test. Unfortunately, the tests were kept behind the counter. Unfortunately, because when we got up to the cashier she asked what we wanted. I pointed discreetly to the pregnancy test. She could not work out what I was pointing at. So I started pointing a little more vigorously. She still could not work out what I was pointing out. Then eventually, I had to say louder than I really wanted to,

"the Clear Blue".

"Oh, the Clear Blue!" she shouted out to the whole world, and smiled.

I know it sounds silly, but I almost died of embarrassment. I didn't want everyone knowing my, our, business.

Still red in the cheeks, I got home and went to the bathroom immediately. I still did not believe I could be even the remotest pregnant. So I didn't think too much about the test as I peed on the stick. However, something odd started to happen. Well, odd when you don't expect something out of the ordinary to happen. Two blue lines began to appear. I shook the stick thinking the test was faulty, but the two blue lines would not go away.

I think I stood in the bathroom for a good five minutes staring at that stick. Stare as I might the results stayed the same. Derrick was talking to my mom in London when I went into our bedroom. I acted all cool, and made my face like the results were negative. I felt bad for pretending but I just wanted to see his expression when I showed him the stick. Well, when he saw that stick he jumped clear of the bed and shouted down the phone to my mom,

"We're pregnant! were pregnant!"

I giggled. It sounded a little odd to hear a man say "We're pregnant!" But I suppose we truly were.

Now I want to share in more detail the things that helped me to accelerate and dance my own fertility journey using only natural remedies and therapies.

Fact Box

Overall research suggests that stress, poor nutrition, weight and infertility are connected. The conclusion is looking after your emotional, physical and spiritual well being can definitely go a long way to helping infertile couples conceive.

Dancing the Seven Principles to Fertility

In Ayurveda I discovered that the mind-body and soul system has a natural balance, and there are certain fundamental principles that are always at play to keep it that way.

I identified these core principles that keep us in balance and wrote about them in my mind-body-soul healing book, "The Seven Principles of Wellness". It was the seven principles concept that I followed to help me leap and dance through the fertility journey. I guide you through the first five, as they proved to be the most important for my successful pregnancy journey.

In Ayurveda the health of our reproductive system is the end result of all that we think, eat and do.

Fact Box

In Ayurvedic medicine mind, body and spiritual health is connected while the health of the ovaries and reproductive system is the end product of our nutritional cycle and good flow of prana (life force) which circulates around the whole mind-body system. The health of overall our mind, body and spiritual system is created by looking after our emotions, food and lifestyle.

Principle 1: The Dance of Inner Knowing

How do you feel about your fertility journey really? Are you facing it with fear? With joy? With love? With an open heart? Or with a sense of inner constriction? How you feel right now about your fertility journey will determine how you embrace its dance. If you are filled with anything but positive uplifting emotions know that you will restrict the reproductive power of your body.

What's the remedy to the fear, the trepidation, the anxiety? As with the Shinto prayer the remedy is to just let go and let be. Where our intention goes is how our lives grow. In terms of the fertility dance, where we place our intention is how the steps follow. The steps will either be heavy, faulty, light, sure, graceful or even a mixture of all of the above. What we want them to really be is joyful. Joyful steps allow us to dance with the universe, knowing that the full power of our bodies, and inner midwife is for us not against us.

Even if you feel stressed about the fertility journey just for a moment allow yourself to let go and trust the universe within and outside of yourself. It is interesting that in Ancient Egypt the Priestess of the Goddess Hathor who governed fertility and child birth (amongst many other areas of life) surrounded the pregnant and birthing woman with positive sounds joyful sounds, that allowed her to be filled with a positive joyful feeling, which in turn allowed the woman to have a positive joyful birthing experience.

Principle 2: The Dance of Emotional Awakening

I believe that the body has this amazing way of letting us know what we are truly thinking. For I have noticed over the years of seeing clients that their body is always there giving messages through their various ailments.

When I did the Shinto prayer something really interesting happened – I became aware that deep down I had not wanted to have a second child. After having my son I constantly said, "I never want another child". So even though I didn't think I was closed to the experience. I truly was not interested in being pregnant again. As a result of a bad experience of being treated badly and emotionally abandoned by his father.

The message and desire not to have another child was embedded right down in the core of my cells. My fertility journey helped me to at last come face to face with the emotions and internal programming that was holding me back from an abundant womb. There was none other than myself truly holding me back.

Open your heart to the possibility that your infertility may be holding a message for you right now. You can do the exercise below to find out and release negative messages, thoughts or feelings you may be holding.

> ## *Worms Hold Memory*
>
> An experiment that proved the body passes on memory involved the most primitive forms of life, a type of worm called Planaria. Scientists kept a group of Planaria in a dark box, flashed a light on them, and then shocked them with electricity. Overtime the worms learned to coil into balls when they saw the light, in anticipation of the electric shock. Then the scientists ground up this group worms and fed them to a new group of worms. They then flashed a light at the new group. The worms coiled into balls! They apparently had learned to hold memory.
>
> Experiment found in book *Medical Science by*
> *Dharma* Singh Khalsa, M.D and Cameron Stauth

Womb Light Healing Exercise

This exercise helps you to identify the message your body is giving you about your fertility journey. All you have to do is simply be in a quiet space and spend a little bit of time releasing your tension through a few inhalations and exhalations.

When you are sufficiently relaxed place your hand on your womb area and tune into that area. Now ask your womb what message does hold for you. This may feel strange, but trust me you will hear an answer come back.

Listen carefully to the reply your body gives, and then respond by letting your womb know that you thank it for its message. Assure it you will do what it has suggests, and that you no longer need the message it is sending in the form of the illness/blockages you are suffering.

I have cured numerous illnesses with this technique for myself and others.

Womb Light Healing Exercise

In this exercise you are going to learn how to send healing light energy to your womb. Spend a few minutes to relax yourself through deep abdominal breathing.

1. Place your right or left hand one inch away from your sacral channel (one inch below your belly button).
2. Ask permission to receive energy from God, Consciousness or whichever name you are comfortable with. Then ask permission to send that light to yourself.
3. Spend five minutes receiving and sending light energy to yourself.
4. Complete the exercise by saying, "thank you".
5. Repeat for up to seven days and afterwards as often as you feel the need to.

Note: this exercise should make you feel quite relaxed. So it's actually a good stress buster too.

Womb Affirmation Exercise

There is a great power in what we say to ourselves. Dr. Emoto Masaru proved this when he took pictures of water crystals, where the water had been exposed to negative and positive statements. The water that had positive statements spoken to it formed beautiful whole crystals, while the opposite was true for the water samples that had negative words spoken to them.

This experiment was further repeated through speaking negative and positive words to cooked rice divided into two jars. One jar had positive words spoken to it and the other didn't. The rice with negative words spoken to it became black and covered in yucky fungi after a few days. The results are recorded in his book "Messages From Water".

My son, Kem Ra, repeated this experiment for his school middle school experiment and got the same results within 14 days. Myself and Derrick shadowed his experiment and got the same results. Below are Kem Ra's Love and Hate Rice experiment results. The white rice is the Love Rice, and the rice with the fungi is the Hate Rice.

Saying positive affirmations to ourselves such as: "I am healthy", "I am well", "I am supported", "I am whole" helps us to nurture and love ourselves gently while getting the results we desire.

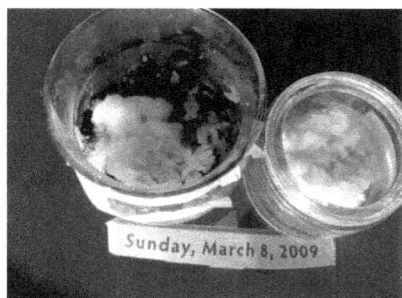

Sunday, March 8, 2009

Principle 3: The Dance of Inner Guidance

Us women are highly intuitive. So learning to trust that female intuition is a good thing that can strengthen all areas of our lives. When we trust our female intuition it very rarely leads us astray. So let's dance with our inner intuition.

Principle 4:The Dance of Body Bliss

As said earlier, our body-mind-and soul balance is maintained and nourished through incorporating certain age old well proven lifestyle practices and tools into our lives. These simple to grasp tools help us to maintain a healthy nourishing energy flow which results in a strong balanced mental, physical and spiritual state.

In Ayurveda our ultimate aim in terms of our internal health is to have what is known as Ojas, good immunity. It is the end result of all the positive things that we do for our bodies, such as healthy eating, lifestyle etc. Ojas is described in the ancient classical text as: *a white fluid that is like the nectar of the Gods. It is sweet, nourishing and life giving.*

The description of Ojas alone is a sure fire way to help encourage us towards health. While its opposite Ama is a sure fire way to scare us totally away from bad health. For Ama is described as: *a thick heavy substance of undigested food matter. It is the end result of a bad diet, lifestyle, emotional and mental habits. It circulates around the body system. Gets stuck in the carrying channels causing a range of feelings and diseases from depression, fatigue, arthritis, diabetes, cancer etc.*

So here are the things that are involved in the Dance of Body Bliss:

Meditation

Meditation is a sure way to help us keep our feet on the Earth and our heads in the Sky. In other words – totally balanced between the physical and ethereal realms that nourish our inner and outer beings.

My first experience of meditation totally convinced me that I wanted to always meditate. That was almost twenty years ago. After being convinced of the calming expansive results of meditation I went onto to successfully share this ancient practice with many others. This sharing experience resulted in my very first book, "A Journey Through Breath".

Some of the recorded benefits of meditation include: lowered blood pressure, lowered pre-menstrual symptoms, reduced stress, 75% of insomniacs can apparently sleep after meditation, more than normal secretion of the youth-related hormone DHEA, chronic pain relief (up to 34 percent of people who meditate have reported reduction of chronic pain), increase in those calming hormones melatonin and serotonin. Let's not forget about those spiritual soulful qualities of meditation: increase clarity, sense of peace, oneness with self that meditation brings.

It is a known fact that mantras can have a powerfully healing effect upon the endocrine system. That is the system that is responsible for our hormonal balance. In one experiment done by a Gurucharan Singh Khalsa, PhD individuals were observed when they were changing a mantra "Sa Ta Na Ma". The PET scan showed that there was a strong shift in brain activities to the right frontal and parietal regions. This shift indicated an improvement in mood and alertness. I share with you my sisters these gentle meditations below to help restore fertility.

Dancing With Gentle Breath Exercise

1. Sit on a straight back chair
2. Place hands palm down on your lap
3. Ensure feet are resting on the ground
4. Sit with a straight posture, achieved by slumping in your chair and pulling yourself up by the waist
5. Breathe in slowly through your nose filling your abdomen up, one inch below your belly button.
6. Pause
7. Breathe out slowly by gently pulling your stomach in and gently allowing the air to be released.

Dancing With Mantra Exercise

1. Sit on a chair or crossed legged on the floor
2. Now you are going to inhale and on your out breath you are going to say OM! Concentrate on your third eye. It's between your eyebrows and is the spot that opens up to give you deep insight and self-discovery. It is also connected to pineal gland which helps to maintain the body's cycle of rest and activity.
3. Inhale again, and on your exhalation you are going to say AHHH! Concentrate on your throat area as you do this. This is known as your throat chakra. It is connected to the thyroid and parathyroid glands which control the body's metabolic rate and mineral levels. On a spiritual and emotional level, the throat

chakra is connected to self-expression.

4. Now inhale once again, and on your exhalation say HUNG! As you do so concentrate on your heart area. This is the home of the heart chakra. It is related to the gland in the thymus which is located above the heart. This is responsible for growth. When we meditate on the heart chakra we not only affect this gland but find our more compassionate loving self.

5. Now, all you have to do is repeat the whole cycle for as long as you feel comfortable. Minimum I have chanted for to great benefit is ten minutes.

Self Massage

In Ayurveda self massage is very important in the maintenance of dancing with our bodies balance. It is part of the Langhana treatment. That is the process of "lightening up". What exactly are we "lightening up?" All the toxins within our system responsible for blocking our health.

I love the self massage routine and have been doing it every day for years. It is free, life giving and doesn't cost a dime.

Some of the further benefits of any type of massage include: preservation of the body's energy; improvement of the blood circulation; improvement of skin tone and texture; removal of toxins out of the body through sweat, urine and mucous; increase of joy and happiness.

Massage is still used to aid the healing of treatment of skin disorders like eczema, blisters, scabies, seborrhea and other conditions like neurasthenia, headaches, sleeplessness, gouty arthritis, polio, obesity and mental disorders. It also increases physical stamina and mental alertness.

Dancing With Self Massage Exercise

1. Wear a swim suit/swimming pants (ladies you can wear a sarong around you; men a towel.)
2. Stand with your legs at shoulder width.
3. Put a little base oil such as: sunflower, almond, olive oil in your hand. With this you will lubricate the part of the body you are about to work on.
4. Begin the massage by starting with your arms. Imagine there are five imaginary lines running down them. The lines start on the inside part of your arm and move outwards. Using small rotational movements begin to follow your imaginary lines in a downward movement. Start from the inside line and work your way out.
5. Now it's time to move onto your waist. Once again, imagine five imaginary lines. This time follow them in upward strokes. Start from your hips and end under your arm pit.
6. Move to your legs. Your imaginary lines are now on the front and back of your legs. Starting with the front of your leg follow those imaginary lines from the inside to the outer edge of your leg. Now do the same for the back of your legs.
7. Now you are going to massage your feet. Sit on a comfortable chair/floor to do so. Your imaginary lines are now on your feet. You will follow them

starting from the heel and outside part of your foot working your way inward and down to your toes

8. Spend five minutes on each body part.
9. Dab of any excess oil with a piece of kitchen towel.

The Dance of Bhumi Drum Energy Dance

During my dance to fertility, all the way through pregnancy, post pregnancy, and in fact every stage of life I have literally danced. I love the drums, I love dancing and I love yoga. Somehow during my pregnancy dance with Omo all of these loves became fused together and became what I now call the Bhumi Drum Energy Dance.

Bhumi Drum Energy Dance is an eclectic nourishing mixture of African traditional dance movements, yoga stretches, spontaneous movements, breath work, self massages, the Seven Principle of Wellness, and the fundamental lessons of life – all woven together through the therapeutic beat of the drums.

The dance works and opens up the chakra system, while nourishing the mind-body and soul. Ultimately, it produces good Ojas (immunity) and helps to transform the dancer into a positive energy flux. I did this energy routine all during my forty day fertility journey. Here I share with you the Yoga segment of Bhumi Drum Energy Dance which is known as: Jala Chandra Namaskar (Water Moon Salutation).

Each movement and stretch is performed like a wave, while making us move energetically within ourselves from our New Moon to our full moon. The feeling of fullness we experience from this movement sequence is the result of the healthy awakening and flow of our nourishing life force energy.

The movements you are going to do are drawn from the Sun and Moon Salutation. They balance the male and female energies of the bodies. The transition between each standing posture is marked by the whining of the hips. This whining of the hips comes from the traditional womb healing dances of the Caribbean and African. It also imitates the life giving rotations of our Mother Earth and movement patterns of subtle energy.

I incorporate Bhumi Drum Energy Dance into many workshop scenarios, to the delight of those who experience.

Just a little knowledge about Yoga. It dates back to thousands of years and is documented within the Yoga Sutra written by sage Patanjali. I have discovered that in many Egyptian pictures there are Yoga postures. In fact Hatha yoga shares the same name as the Egyptian Goddess Hathor.

There is more to Yoga than just its physical poses. There are eight petals of this ancient tradition: ethical discipline (yama), internal ethical observances (niyama), poses (asana), breath control (pranayama), sensory control and withdrawal (pratyahara), concentration (dharma), meditation (dhyana), and blissful absorption (samadhi). These petals awaken us like a beautiful flower.

In yoga, the body is said to be made up of different layers of energy sheaths. There are five in all. The aim of life and self-development is to integrate these sheaths to bring into being a sense of wholeness. The body is our outer most sheaths which manifest as physical form. The others are: the energetic body, mental body, intellectual body and the soul body. It is the physical body which encompasses all the other sheaths. The sheaths are not as delineated as we have made it sound. Each one is part of the other. There must be full integration from the soul to the outer physical body and from the physical body back to the soul. In this way we are fully functional in life and infused with consciousness in all that we do.

In terms of the physical movement of Yoga or any energy system like yoga it is with the integration of all sheaths of the body and in mind, which one stretches. We allow ourselves to not only be active in life but "consciously active," as Yoga master B.KS Iyengar succinctly states in his book *Light on Life.*

The Jala Chandara Namaskar (Water Moon Salutation) segment of Bhumi Drum Energy Dance draws Moon Namaskar The Sun Salutation. It is a series of yoga poses performed in a graceful flow linked by breath. Allowing us to achieve the balance we crave for on this journey.

The great thing about the Jala Chandar Namaskar section of Bhumi Drum Energy Dance is that you don't have to bend like spaghetti. You just bend to your own body's stretch capacity. If you want a taste of my style of yoga all you have to do is whine those hips in between each movement

Jala Chandra Namaskar (Water Moon Salutation) You Will Need

- Comfortable clothing suitable for stretching and

moving
- A calm place where you won't be distracted or disturbed
- A yoga mat or folded blanket

Step 1.Mountain Pose: Stand at the front of your mat in the Mountain Pose, with your feet hip-width apart and your weight evenly distributed between them, your spine erect, and your arms at your sides.

Step 2. Arms Reaching Upward: Inhale into the Arms Reaching Upward Pose, extending your arms overhead, bringing your palms together, and expanding your chest.

Step 3. Standing Forward Bend: Exhale into the Standing Forward Bend, bringing your chest toward your thighs and your hands toward the floor.

Step 4. Lung Pose: Inhale into the Lunge Pose, placing your hands on the mat on either side of your right foot as you lunge your left leg straight back behind you. Expand your chest as you lengthen your spine.

Step 5: Plank Pose: Exhale into the Plank Pose, stepping your right leg back so your feet are now side by side. Look straight at the floor, keeping your arms extended and your body straight. Hold this pose for 3 to 5 full breaths.

Step 6. Kneel & lower head. Exhale, slowly dropping your knees to the floor. Untuck your toes, bring your hips back to your heels, and lower your head to the floor with your arms still extended in front of you.

Step 7. Get on all fours: Inhale, slowly bringing yourself up on all fours.

Step 8. Lower chest & chin: Exhale, slowly bending your elbows and lowering your chest and chin to the floor so your hands, knees, and feet are touching the mat.

Step 9. Upward Facing Dog: Inhale into the Upward Facing Dog Pose, pushing your head and ribcage up off the mat by fully extending your arms as you press the tops of your feet into the ground. Your thighs and hips should rise a few inches above the mat.

Step 10. Downward Facing: Do exhale into the Downward Facing Dog Pose, tucking your toes and lifting your hips up and back so that you're bearing your weight on the balls of your feet. This should create an upside-down V shape with your body. Relax your neck and allow the weight of your head to lengthen your spine.

Step 11. Lung Pose: Inhale into the Lung Pose again, stepping your left foot forward.

Step 12. Standing Forward Bend: Exhale into the Standing Forward Bend again, stepping your right foot forward next to your left foot so your weight is on both feet.

Step 13. Arms Reaching Upward: Inhale into the Arms Reaching Upward Pose again.

Step 14. Mountain Pose: Exhale, completing the Sun Salutation by returning to the Mountain Pose.

Sleep

Sleep allows us to deeply restore ourselves. In a 2002 poll, over 80% of American adults believed that not getting enough sleep leads to poor performance at work, risk of injury, poor health and difficulty getting on with others. Recent research also indicates that sleeping impacts on aging, diabetes, and overall health.

Sleep is regulated by two brain processes. One is the restorative process; the other the process that controls the timing of sleep. The first kicks in according to how many waking hours we have. The more hours we have had awake the stronger the urge to sleep is. The second process helps us to feel sleepy during the night time and awake in the day. It is governed by the circadian biological clock that is located in the part of the brain known as SCN (Suprachiasmatic nucleus). The SCN is influenced by light so that we naturally tend to get sleepy at night when it is dark and are active during the day when it is light. The circadian clock also regulates day-night cycles of most body functions ensuring that the right levels of body functioning occur at night when we are sleeping. The hormones are secreted, blood pressure is lowered and the kidney function changed. Research also indicates that memory is consolidated during sleep. It is said that establishing a regular bed and wake time helps promote sleep by getting us in sync with our circadian clock so that we experience all the stages of sleep.

Getting enough sleep most definitely impacts on the quality of our lives. We perform better the following day, we feel less sleepy during the day time, and we experience a greater sense of overall wellness. By the way, day sleeping promotes obesity. In Ayurveda sleep is known as "nidra" and getting enough of it is said to promote: happiness, nourishment, strength, sexual potency, knowledge and longevity.

In Ayurvedic medical text it is further stated that keeping very late night times promotes increased Vata and all that goes with it: excessive dryness of the skin, internal organs, and a feeling of living on our nerves. On the other hand day time sleeping increases the heavy earth energy of Kapha causing a feeling of heaviness, lethargy in the body, and weight gain. Traditionally day sleep is said to be only beneficial when one is: exhausted by heat, excess speech, walking for long distances, sexual activities, anger, grief and fear. It is also good for those who are aged, young, debilitated, wounded, suffering from indigestion or habituated through work routine to sleeping during the day.

So what is enough sleep? This varies from person to person but 7-9 hours of sleep time leaves our souls feeling restored. To promote good quality sleep:

- Avoid caffeine, nicotine close to bedtime
- Avoid alcohol

- Exercise regularly but do gentle exercises in the evening as the body is naturally winding down
- Have a healthy balanced diet and lifestyle
- Create a sleep conducive environment that is dark, quiet, cool and comfortable

The Dance of Yoga Nidra Exercise

Restoring our wombs, mind-body and souls can successfully be done through Yoga Nidra, The ancient yoga practice of getting enough restorative zzzzs.

1. Lie on a flat surface
2. Do your Gentle Breath exercise (see meditation section) for up to fifteen minutes
3. Now you are going to work through the chakra colors. Keep on gently inhaling and exhaling. As you do so spend a few minutes breathing and circulating each the colors through your body. How do you do this? You imagine the air is filled with the color. You inhale it and imagine it flowing from your head and all the way around your body. As it does so feel it filling you up completely and utterly. On each exhalation you release all the tension and stress.

   The colors in the order you will breath them are: *Red, orange, yellow, light blue, dark blue, and purple/gold.* The chakra chart below will tell you which chakra each color relates to. **Be warned** you might fall asleep by the time you hit yellow. I normally do.

Chakra Chart

The crown chakra is purple/gold. On top the head and near the crown it governs our higher spiritual connection. It governs the pituitary gland that controls the whole endocrine (hormone) system. The entire cerebral cortex is influenced by centre. This chakra governs physical balance and movement. Problems with this chakra can lead to a feeling of being uncoordinated, depressed and a draining feeling of being dissatisfied

The brow chakra is dark blue. It is located between the eyebrows. This is the site of the third eye which is said to give us deep insight and intuition. It is here we gain our ability to be imaginative. This charka is connected to the pineal gland that maintains cycles of rest and activity. It is also connected to the carotid plexus of nerves. Problems with this charka can lead to a feeling of being disorientated and blocked.

The throat chakra is light blue. It is located in the Base of the throat it rules our ability to communicate with others and our inner self. It also governs creativity. Thyroid and parathyroid glands which controls the body's metabolic rate and mineral levels. The pharyngeal plexus are found here. Problems in this area manifest as the inability to be creative and express the authentic self.

The heart chakra is green or pink. It is in the center of the chest. It rules the heart and our ability to show true compassion and love. This chakra regulates our interaction with the outside world. It is related to the gland in the thymus, located above the heart. It is vital for growth. When this chakra is blocked feelings are withheld. Too open it leads to physical and emotional exhaustion.

The solar plexus is yellow. It is situated below the sternum. It governs our feelings of self-power and individuality. This chakra is associated with the adrenal glands and the pancreas. It is named after the complex of nerves found here and is connected to the lumbar vertebrae. A blocked or impaired chakra can lead to difficult relationships where the person feels out of control and dominated by others. The individual could also end up being the dominator.

The sacral chakra is orange. It is located two finger widths below the navel. It governs our creativity, emotional and physical security. Blocked emotions are re-balanced by this chakra. It is related to the sacral vertebrae in the spine, the sacral plexus of nerves and the sex glands. When out of balance it affects our creativity and expression of our authentic emotions.

The base chakra is red. It lies in the perineum, the space between the genitals and anus. When it functions properly we feel passionate, motivated, clear, grounded and confident about life. Out of balance we lack the courage and energy to live our dreams. It is related to the adrenals, testicles, ovaries and physical body.

Principle 5: The Dance of Body Nourishment

In Ayurveda keeping to the principles of the nourishment cycle helps us to hold on and enhance good health. In "Seven Principles of Wellness" I call this cycle *The Simple Cycle of Nutrition*. Now that is my term for what Ayurveda talks of in terms of nourishing the body. *The Simple Cycle* of Nutrition goes something like this.

It involves knowing that our beautiful bodies are made up of 60 trillion cells. Each of these cells form together to make our tissues which in turn forms our organs.

In *The Simple Cycle of Nutrition* the body must nourish our seven principle tissues: plasma, blood, fat, muscle, bone, bone marrow, and egg/sperm. These tissues are fed from food essence formed in the stomach. Our food essence is made up of the food we have ingested through our mouths. If the food essence is good the tissues fed are said to be well nourished. On the other hand, if the food essence is not good (filled with partially digested food matter known as toxins) the opposite is true. If the food essence our tissues receive is "bad" then the result equals blocked elimination channels, malnourishment of cells, tissues, and organs – leading to disease.

In *The Simple Cycle of Nutrition* it is not only what we take into our body which is crucial to the good formation of nourishing food essence but how we take those things into our bodies. So eating fast leads to undigested food matter and therefore "bad" food essence. Eating after 6pm (especially heavy meals) leads to undigested food matter and "bad" food matter. I think you get the picture.

Understanding *The Simple Cycle of Nutrition* is easy, can revolutionize and accelerate our ability to restore mind-body-soul and fertility health. The Simple Cycle of Nutrition involves the following principles:

Do not Over Eat

Overeating is one of the major causes of disease both mild and severe in the body. Our digestion is a delicate chemical balance. Anything that upsets that causes food to be partially digested resulting in the formation of toxic food essence. As you read earlier, when the food essence of the body is toxic then it: creates illness in vulnerable parts of the body, causes malnourishment of cellular tissue and blocked elimination channels. The result is not nice.

Ayurveda states that overeating causes Mandagni (slowed and impaired digestion). In the ancient Vedic medical *Charaka Samita* it is said that the "Correct quantity of food increases life span". Our innate body intelligence lets us know this anyway. I know when I over eat I feel awful. I am sure there are few people that could claim to feel vital, alive and ready to go for it after over filling their stomachs. I saw an interesting article recently on an 8 year old British boy who weighed 218LBs. He was so overweight that British social workers wanted to take the boy into protected custody "for his own protection." His mother who appeared to be quite slim herself gave away the secret to his size "he eats double or triple what a normal eight year old would". So do Sumo Wrestlers.

But how much is too much? In reality food quantity is different for every individual. But I believe we all know when we have overeaten. For those of us who want to be doubly sure, Ayurveda reveals we should visualize the stomach and divide it into three imaginary compartments. We should fill one with healthy carbs and proteins like rice, and vegetables. The second with liquids like water, soup, juices. The third kept empty for air or gases. Or just make sure your meal fits in the cup of your hands. In Ayurvedic medicine it states there are further indicators of overeating: obstruction in the heart, pain in sides, and heaviness in abdomen. When you have overeaten it is also uncomfortable to lie, sit, breath, laugh or talk. You will also feel as though there is a loss of strength.

Do not Under eat

Many books mention the problems about overeating, but it is also important that we do not under eat. Over eating means that we are over nourishing ourselves and when we under eat we do the opposite. Under eating provides the body with: no satisfaction of hunger and thirst, here is loss of strength, loss of immunity, damage to mental functions and damage to sense organs. It is important that our body receives the nutrients it requires for a sense of total wellness.

Do not eat too soon after meals

Eating meals too close together causes food to be only partially digested and leads to fermentation in the intestinal track. There should be four hours, at least, between each meal.

Eat a balanced food plate

The statistics vary slightly as to what a balanced food plate looks like but if you aim for 40% healthy carbohydrates, 40 % healthy protein, and 20% wholesome fat you should be on the right track.

Do not eat raw foods

The west has taken very much to the idea that raw food is best. However, the ancient Indian medical system says that raw food can hamper the digestive power. The reality is that for most of us our digestive power is very weak. Lightly steamed food or liquid drinks are a good way to still eat nutrient rich food.

Eat food at body temperature

Overly hot or overly cold food does one thing – stagnates the digestive fire. Impairment of the digestive system leads to undigested food matter (toxins) which float around the system creating disease.

Know your own body clock. Eat accordingly

Have you noticed the sun rises and sets at a certain time each day? When I lived in the Islands I became even more sensitized to this fact. The sun would rise brilliantly every morning and set brilliantly every evening. The rhythms of nature are reflected within our own bodies.

From 6-10am our body is sleepy, heavy and waking up to the world. This fact stretches to our digestive system. Between 10 am and 2pm the body is feeling more dynamic especially as it passes 12am. Our digestive system is also more fired up along with our brain power and ability to do. Between 2pm and 6pm the body is beginning to slow down and go into rest mode. The closer it gets to 6pm is the more restful it starts to become. This is the period when the digestive system and the mind begin to feel more sluggish. Between 6pm and 10pm the body is now at rest, the digestive system has more or less closed for the night. The latter will not digest anything too heavy. Between 10pm and 2am the body begins the process of assimilation of our thoughts, day and food matter. Once we reach 2am to 6am the body is involved in creative thinking, visions and dreams. It is definitely not thinking about digesting our even assimilating food but more moving things to where they need to be. At 6am this cycle begins all over again.

So what happens if you go against your natural body clock? Well imagine eating a heavy meal after 6pm. From what has been said you know the body is no longer digesting anything (particularly heavy food matter). This should tell us that what is eaten after this time remains undigested in the stomach. The result - body toxicity and weight gain. Also eating a heavy meal between 6pm to 10pm slows down the digestion, diminishes the digestive power, and causes fermentation and formation of toxins in the stomach and thus body.

Understanding and working with the body clock is one of the major secrets to good health and weight loss.

Eat food that has been properly combined

Ayurveda has much to say about food combining. It is said that food combining should be done with the utmost of care, as bad food combining can cause bad health through impairment of the digestive system.

It is said two or more food items of similar quality should not be combined. So milk has a sweet quality and sugar is sweet so these two are hazardous to mix. Milk and fish should never combine. Milk and fruit is another combination sure to cause putrefaction in the system. So all that advice about putting a banana with breakfast cereal is a disastrous idea.

The ancient principle of food combining was brought to further light by what became a popular diet –

The Hay Diet by Dr. William Howard Hay. Dr. Hay introduced food combining in 1911. His basic premise was that there is one underlying cause for health problems and that is the wrong chemical condition in the body which is acidity.

This acid condition results in a lowering of the body's vital alkaline reserve, the depletion of which causes toxemia or auto intoxication (basically internal poisoning).

Dr. Hay classified foods into three types according to their chemical requirements for efficient digestion and their digestive by product. These were: -

1. Fruits and vegetables: Alkali forming as final end product in the stomach. Note even acid tasting fruits such as lemons yield alkaline salts in the body.
2. Concentrated proteins such as meat, game, fish, eggs or cheese. These foods are acid forming in their final end products in the body.
3. Concentrated carbohydrates or starch foods, which are acid forming. These include grains, bread, and all foods containing flour, all sugars and foods containing sugars (sucrose), but not the naturally occurring sugars found in fruit.

Dr. Hay's rules for food combining which reflects ancient principles of good food combining are:

1. Starches and sugars should not be eaten with proteins and acid fruits at the same meal.
2. Vegetables, salads and fruits (whether acid or sweet) if correctly combined should form the major part of the diet.

3. Proteins, starches and fats should be eaten in small quantities.
4. Only whole grains and unprocessed starches should be used and all refined and processed foods should be eliminated from the diet.
5. Not less than four hours between starch and protein meals.
6. Milk does not combine well with food and should be kept to a minimum.
7. Don't mix foods that fight. So proteins can be mixed with neutral (alkaline foods), proteins and starches should never be mixed together, starches and neutral (alkaline) foods can be mixed.

Eat food that has been prepared right

Over frying, barbecuing, and microwaving food kills the nutritional value of food. Barbecuing is known to produce carcinogenic. If you have to fry it is better to quickly stir fry in a wok. It is really better to steam food where possible and not to overcook it. Researchers in Sweden found that acrylamide, a chemical which is classified as a probable human carcinogen and is known to cause benign and stomach tumors in animal test, was formed when carbohydrate-rich foods such as potatoes, rice or cereals are heated and overheated. The study found that an ordinary bag of crisp may contain up to 500 times more of the substance than the top level allowed in drinking water by the World Health Organization (WHO). While French fries contained up to 100 times the one microgram per liter maximum permitted by the WHO in drinking water.

I remember once when I was trying to find myself and did a second degree in Conservation (which I never completed). I had to do an essay on radiation. This essay led me to a book which spoke about the powerful radioactive effect microwaves have on food. It further went on to explain how microwaves destroy the delicate chemical bonds of food. For a long time after that I did not use a microwave again and discouraged the use of microwaves by my family.

When I read Dr. Emoto, author of *The True Power of Water*, findings about the effects of microwaves on food I was intrigued (please read the first Principle of Wellness to read more about this amazing man, his revolutionary experiments and findings). He took distilled water which he has proven would normally form beautiful crystals and heated it in a microwave for fifteen seconds. The water formed no crystals only "grotesque shapes.

From his experiments Mr. Emoto concluded "the electromagnetic waves of microwave ovens are quite strong. By exposing water to the waves for just fifteen seconds, the good Hado (energy) of the distilled water was destroyed completely. He then took a homemade burger and compared three different cooking methods by using a Hado (energy measuring) machine. The methods used were: frying or microwaving for a normal amount of time (two minutes); microwaving for an excessive amount of time (three minutes). Needless to say the burger that had been pan fried fared the best, while the burger that had been exposed to excessive microwave waves fared the worst.

Enjoy local food

When I lived in the UK there was a growing push to eat food that was grown by local growers. Recently when I lived in Trinidad I always tried to buy food that was locally grown. My mother and I did a little experiment where we compared the taste of locally grown veg and fruit to those that had been brought into the country from the US and other places. The results were interesting and I suppose to be expected. We found that the locally grown fruit and vegetables tasted better, and sweeter. Much research has shown that food that is not locally produced and has to be brought into a country goes through a process that causes the food to lose much of its nutritional value. In other words it becomes energetically depleted.

Chew well

Chewing food slowly is to eat with total appreciation. When we eat with appreciation we aid in the production of good nutritional food essence. Eating food slowly begins the digestive process. It stimulates the digestive system into action and the digestive enzyme, amylase, moistens the chewed food breaking it down even further.

Eat in a social environment

Have you ever tried eating when you are feeling seriously uptight? It's difficult, isn't it? One of the most ancient principles to good digestion is "to eat in a social setting". Social means to eat with company. If you have to eat alone do not sit in front of the TV or while doing other activities like talking on the phone. Social also means to eat in a relaxed atmosphere. This puts a no on eating in the full height of negative emotions, eating when stressed, or when just feeling seriously tense. Just a little note on eating in front of the TV. Overwhelming evidence has shown that this activity is linked to the growing rate of obesity in society.

Cook with love

I remember once dining in a London restaurant with my family where the food always tasted good. It was a small family owned business where the husband managed and the wife cooked. The food was so delicious it was hard pushed to get a table at this restaurant. I have many fond memories of eating there. There was another restaurant just around the corner from our regular one where the food always tasted bad. It was a bigger more faceless establishment where the staff was quite unfriendly. We ate there twice and never again.

What was the difference with these two places – love? Food cooked with love is vibrationally good food. It is food that taste "sweet" to the palate and goes down well in the stomach. So let's try to avoid cooking when we are angry, upset or feeling negative. Let's also try to avoid eating at food places that have not cooked with our best health interest at heart.

Remember the rice experiment mentioned earlier on in the book. It shows that love does make a difference.

Weight & Fertility

While studies connecting obesity to ovulation are not news, a study led by Dr. Van der Steeg, a medical researcher at the Academic Medical Center in The Netherlands shows that even women who regularly ovulate experience sub-fertility when their BMI (body mass index) is in the overweight or obese category. Someone experiencing sub-fertility has a lower than normal chance of becoming pregnant, but unlike women suffering from infertility, spontaneous pregnancy is still likely. Also recent research have shown that overweight men are not as fertile as there slimmer counterparts.

As we dance with the nourishment of the body we may also desire to embrace the Dance of Detoxification. In Ayurveda and mind-body research detoxification helps us to clean out all the bad stuff from our blood and system. In Eastern and other form of world traditional healing systems medicine toxins are the culprits behind disease. Now that is emotional or physical toxins.

When to Detox

Traditionally the time to cleanse and re-balance our bodies and minds are: at the end of each seasonal cycle, moving from one country to another either permanently or just for holiday, when we are ill, when we are recovering from illness, when we have over indulged, when we are making a move from one life experience to another, when we are in recovery from emotional trauma or stagnation.

How many days should we detox? That depends on how severe the feeling of being out of balance is. The general rule of thumb you can apply is when: you feel tired, bloated, irritable, or lack focus a minimum of a three day detox is good. If you have merely over indulged for a day or two or just want to get back on track a one day detox goes a long way too. If you have any medical conditions ask your doctor for advice before you go on a detox.

Symptoms of Detoxing

You may experience hunger pangs, fatigue and tiredness when you do a detox. This is normal as the body is clearing itself of years of gunk. The good thing is, after wards you will feel great. Ensure you drink plenty of water during your detox. It is also important that you do it at a time when you will not be rushing around with a busy work schedule. Detoxing is a perfect time to take quiet time for yourself and to renew your spirits. It is also a good thing to do while you go through your healing journey. As we "lighten up" through detox we begin to have a greater sense of self awareness. We can feel our pores and we begin to sense our consciousness fully through the eyes of our body and cells again.

A Japanese Study on Fasting

In a recent Japanese study on fasting we can see the great benefits that doing a detox brings. It showed that fasting therapy proved 87% effective in curing or ameliorating a wide variety of psychosomatic and mental diseases. The study, conducted by Haruyosi Yamamoto, Jinichi Suzuki and Yuichi Yamauchi of the Department of Psychosomatic Medicine, Nagamachi Branch Hospital, Tohoku University School of Medicine, Sendai, Japan, involved 380 patients who underwent a complete fast for 10 days.

Throughout the fasting period, patients lived in an ashram-like atmosphere conducive to self-analysis and relaxation, and free from the usual distractions of daily life. Patients were accommodated in private rooms, but newspapers, radio and television were prohibited, as well as all non-medical visitors. In this way experimenters preserved the optimal conditions for mental introspection, enhanced self-awareness and physical purification which enabled the patients to successfully recognize and come to grips with their problems without outside distractions or interference.

During the course of therapy, patients were encouraged to drink a minimum of 1000 mils. (10 glasses) of water per day to maintain tissue hydration and to promote internal cleansing and elimination of wastes from the body tissues. In addition, 500 mils. of 5% pentose solution, containing various vitamins and small amounts of essential amino acids, was administered intravenously every day. This provides the body with a minimal level of nutrition, without activating the digestive process. It thus allows the self-purification of the fasting process to proceed unimpeded for the 10 day period, without placing excessive demands on patients unfamiliar with fasting prior to the experiment.

Return to normal diet was strictly supervised over 5 days after the conclusion of the 10 day fasting period, to ensure that metabolic and physiological re-adaption to a normal diet and lifestyle occurred without mishap. The return to normal diet followed the order of fluid diet, soft diet, then ordinary Japanese style diet.

A Simple Effective Detox Plan

There are a million ways to detox but here's a really simple effective one. Make sure to do a castor oil purge before you start. You can purchase castor oil from your local store. Just read the instructions on the bottle. Make sure you don't take it when you're pregnant!

o   Put aside three days to a week
o   Cut out all refined carbohydrates
o   Eat lots of salad, steamed vegetables, and soups
o   Drink lots of fresh juice
o   If you are working make sure you load up on your salad and steamed vegetables

The Dance of Juicing

Juicing is a powerful, simple and cost effective way to get in a power punch of numerous minerals and vitamins. I have one juice that I change just like those 5 way dresses. It works a treat and real tasty and good.

Tips for Juicing

- Try to buy organic fruit or veg
- Before juicing wash fruit and veg thoroughly
- Pre-chop fruit and veg. Bag in a sandwich bag and stick in the fridge. This pre-prep saves on a lot of time
- Always water juice down with choice from the following: coconut milk, coconut water, water, rice milk, soy milk or almond milk. (Try various ones for different taste)
- Juice should be drank within half an hour of juicing. However, if you want to preserve the juice turn it into a shake by adding honey and non-dairy milk
- Add ginger to juice for a kick and to fire up the digestive system
- Adding chlorophyll/blue green algae or wheat germ to juice gives it that extra green power most of us need.
- Grating nutmeg into juice also gives it a wonderful taste
- DON'T BE SCARED TO EXPERIMENT!

•

Carrot Chaser Basic

Juice:
4-5 carrots
1-2 apples
½ beet root
1 tablespoon of ginger
Pinch of cayenne pepper
Dilute with water
Pour in glass and enjoy!

Caribbean Tropical Carrot Chaser

Juice:
4-5 carrots
1-2 apples
½ beet root
1 tablespoon of ginger pinch of cayenne pepper
mix coconut milk and honey to taste.

Tropical Green Power Chaser

Juice:

4-5 carrots
1-2 apples
½ beet root
½ bunch of spinach
½ cucumbers
1 tablespoon of ginger pinch of cayenne pepper
Mix coconut milk and honey to taste
You can add 1 tablespoon blue green
algae/chlorophyll powder

More Food Tips

Vitamin and Mineral Booster

Also try to include the following vitamins and minerals in your diet:

- *Vitamin C and Antioxidants:* these vitamins prevent sperm defects and boost sperm motility. They also reduce stress on your eggs and reproductive organs.
- *Zinc:* zinc deficiencies have been linked with reduced testosterone and semen levels.
- *Calcium and Vitamin D*: A daily, therapeutic dose of

these nutrients have been shown to help increase male fertility.

- *Pre-Natal Vitamins*: at least for six months before you plan to become pregnant

Foods to definitely avoid

- *Alcohol:* alcohol can reduce your fertility levels by up to 50%. It can also decrease sperm count and increase the production of abnormal sperm.
- *Caffeine:* caffeine, found in coffee, teas, cola, and chocolate, has been shown to reduce both male and female fertility levels.
- xenoestrogens are estrogens found in environmental chemicals and pesticides. Produce and other foods can have high levels of xenoestrogens, which, if ingested, may disturb your balance of hormones. Imbalanced hormones are often the cause of fertility issues.

Dancing the Path of Herbal Medicine for Fertility

Herbal medicine formed a major part of my growing up. I remember seeing Tanti (my great grandmother) picking herbs from the garden in Trinidad (in the days I had the privilege to spend a few years of youth with her).

In London where I was born and grew up, I remember my mother growing many herbs and treating us children with natural remedies. Such was the Island way. Therefore turning to the power of herbal medicine during my abundant pregnancy journey was a natural option for me. No one had to convince me about there healing power. I already had experience as to their therapeutic effect.

In Ayurveda herbal medicine is an integral part in healing the mind-body and soul system. On my BS Ayurvedic and Complementary Medicine course I was further exposed to the deepened study of herbal medicine. To say that herbal remedies and teas can be useful in the fertility and pregnancy dance is an understatement. Let's just say, I lived on herbal teas and remedies every step of this beautiful dance. I feel a great joy to be able to share the knowledge of simple therapeutic use herbal remedies within these pages.

Herbal Remedies

Infusions: Where the herb is steeped in simmering water from five to twenty minutes. The end result is potent and often bitter. An infusion should be strained. Most infusions are made with at least one to two rounded teaspoons of fresh herb per cup of water. The dosage for infusions is usually one-half cup three times a day.

Decoctions: Are made in the same way as an infusion. They are reserved for the bark, root or berry of the herb. The dosage for making a decoction is usually one teaspoon of herb per cup of water, three times a day.

Tinctures: Are made by soaking herbs in an alcohol solution of 25 percent alcohol and 75% water. The alcohol helps to draw out the potency of the herb. To make your own tinctures use one ounce of dried herbs in five ounces of distilled alcohol (brandy, rum, vodka or even cider vinegar). Place in a bottle, keep in a cool dark place, and shake the mixture every few days for six weeks. The dosage of the tincture depends on the herbs being used.

Extracts: These are made by distilling some of the alcohol of the tincture and leaving a more potent solution behind. The dosage of the extract depends on the herb being used.

Powdered Herbs: The dried herb is ground into a powder and placed in tablet or capsule form. The dosage for powdered herbs depends on the herb being used.

Remember some herbs can interact with certain conventional medications so be sure to consult your doctor before use. Also start of by drinking low dosages of the herb. In the world of herbal remedies more does not necessarily mean better. Signs that you have taken too high a dosage of the herb include: stomach upset, headaches and nausea one to two hours after taking. If you get any of these symptoms it is a good idea to stop taking the herb or try a lower dosage.

The herbs I recommend here are taken in the form of herbal infusions. You can also buy them in their tincture form too. You can use the herbs as single remedies or combine them. Store excess tea in the fridge.

Herbal Remedies Fertility Dance

For Hormonal Balance

Our bodies work in a fine balancing act. Oftentimes issues with fertility are caused by faulty hormonal balance. So many things can knock our hormonal system of track. There are herbs which can help to get it back on track.

Chasteberry

Is renowned as a hormonal normalizer. This fragrant plant is a deciduous shrub which grows to varied heights. It has clusters of bluish-pink scented blooms, which become small, dark purple aromatic berries. The Latin name of the plant is Agnus-castus. During Ancient Greek times, Athenian women would put the leaves on their couches during sacred rites to the Goddess Ceres.

Chasteberry has the effect of stimulating and normalizing the pituitary gland functions, especially its progesterone function. Recent findings confirm that vitex helps restore a normal estrogen-to-progesterone balance.

The greatest use of Chasteberry lies in normalizing the activity of female sex hormones and it is thus indicated for dysmenorrhoea, premenstrual stress and other disorders related to hormone function. It is especially beneficial during menopausal changes. In a similar way it may be used to aid the body to regain a natural balance after the use of the birth control pill.

In the late 1950's, in a study of 51 women who had heavy bleeding and excessively short menstrual cycles, 65% of those who took a remedy made with Chasteberry showed improvement. About 47% of the women were entirely cured (those over 20 years old seemed to have the highest cure rate). Other problems that vitex can help include fibroid cysts that occur in the smooth muscle tissue, or subserous areas. It can also help to decrease menopausal symptoms and increase milk flow.

For Womb Toning

There are many instances such as fatigue, illness, stress, a range of gynecological conditions, over use of medications which can leave our whole system debilitated including the womb and whole reproductive system. There are several herbs which are renowned for their womb and reproductive toning effects. These include: Blue Cohosh, Black Cohosh, Patridge Berry, Life Root and Black Haw. You can use these herbs on their own or in combinations.

Blue Cohosh

Blue Cohosh (Caulophylum thalictroides) is a uterine tonic, emmenagogue, anti-spasmodic, anti-rheumatic and diuretic. It was used by Native Americans for smooth labor. It is a wonderful uterine tonic that may be used in all situations where there is a weakness or loss of uterine tone. It also may be used at any time during pregnancy. As an anti-spasmodic it diverts the threat of miscarriage, alleviates false labor pains. As an emmenagogue it brings on suppressed menstruation. During labor it helps in a smooth delivery. Precaution: Even though it is said that Blue Cohosh is useful throughout the pregnancy journey. It is better to be on the safe side and use it in the latter part of the pregnancy.

Black Cohosh

Black Cohosh (Cimicifuga racemosa), is a powerful yet gentle remedy: Emmenagogue, anti-spasmodic, alterative, nervine, hypotensive. It is renowned as a relaxant and normalizer of the female reproductive system. It may be used to ease painful or delayed menstruation; as well as ovarian cramps or cramping pain in the womb will be relieved by Black Cohosh. Which makes it helpful for easing the pain of labor. As a relaxing nervine it may be used in many situations where such an agent is needed. Precaution: Black Cohosh should not be used in the earlier part of pregnancy.

Patridge Berry

Partridge Berry (Mitchelle repens) is a good remedy for preparing the uterus and whole body for a good birth. It is also a good uterine tonic. *Usage:* Make an infusion with 1 teaspoon of the herb. Drink three times a day.

Life Root

Life Root (Senecio aureus) is a great uterine tonic which also has anti-inflammatory, diuretic, Emmenagogue, expectorant properties. As a uterine tonic Life Root may be used safely where strengthening of the uterus and reproductive organs are required. It is a good tonic for general debilitation of the body system. Usage: 1-3 teaspoons of dried herb to one cup of water make as an infusion. Drink three times a day.

Black Haw

This herb (Viburnum prunifolium) is an anti-spasmodic, nervine, hypotensive, and astringent. It is a powerful relaxant of the uterus and is used for dysmenorrhoea, false labor pains and threatened miscarriages. Its relaxant properties make it powerful in reducing high blood pressure. *Usage*: 1 teaspoon of dried herb in one cup of water. Make as an infusion. Drink three times a day.

Nettles

Nettles (urtica dioica) is an astringent, diuretic, tonic, hypotensive herb. With its high levels of minerals, chlorophyll, iron and vitamin C it is a good all round tonic which strengthens and supports the whole body. Throughout Europe it is used as a spring tonic and gentle detoxifying remedy. Native American women believed that drinking Nettle tea during pregnancy would strengthen the uterus. They also believed it would stop uterine bleeding after childbirth. Usage: 1 teaspoon of dried herb in one cup of water. Make as an infusion. Drink three times a day.

For Emotional Balance

Emotional problems, tension and anxiety, or the just wanting to conceive a child can all produce physical and physiological blockages to conception. When this is the case there are herbs which can help ease much of the stress away. These include Skull Cap, and Vervain.

Skullcap

Skullcap (Scutellaria laterifolia) is a nervine tonic, anti-spasmodic, hypotensive. It is widely used as a herb to relieve states of nervous tension. The beauty in skullcap is that it relaxes the nervous system and nourishes it all at the same time. It can ease all symptoms of tension and is great for relieving the symptoms of pre-menstrual tension. *Usage*: 2 teaspoon of dried herb in one cup of water. Make as an infusion. Drink three times a day.

Vervain

Vervain (Verbena officinalis) is a nervine tonic, sedative, anti-spasmodic, diaphoretic, hypotensive, galactagogue, hepatic. It is a herb that will strengthen the nervous system whilst relaxing any tension and stress. It can be used to ease depression and sadness, especially when this follows illness such as influenza. As a diaphoretic it can be used in the early stages of fevers. As a hepatic remedy it will be found to be helpful in easing inflammation of the gall-bladder and jaundice. *Usage*: 2 teaspoon of dried herb in one cup of water. Make as an infusion. Drink three times a day.

Fertility Tea Combinations

Here is a possible combination for a Fertility Tea recipe you can try:

Ingredients
Womb Tonic: Blue Cohosh
Hormonal Balancer: Chaste Berry
Nervine: Skullcap and Nervine
Overall Tonic: Nettles

Directions
Put two teaspoons of each herb in a small saucepan of water.
Simmer for five minutes
Strain
Stir in milk
Sweeten with a little bit of honey
Store excess in fridge
Drink three times a day

My All Purpose Tea

Here it is. That tea I told you I use for almost everything.

Ingredients
Calmative: Chamomile
Blood Tonic: Yellow Dock, Red Clover
Overall Tonic: Nettles

Directions
Put two teaspoons of each herb in a small saucepan of water.
Simmer for five minutes
Strain
Stir in milk
Sweeten with a little bit of honey
Store excess in fridge
Drink three times a day

The Dance of Fertility: A Few More Facts

The Dance of Statistics

I discovered that many couples experience fluctuations between fertility and infertility. Many couples do not even realize they may be experiencing a period of infertility when they are not trying for a child. They mainly become aware of this when they begin to try. It is said at least 85 percent of couples will conceive within a year. The other fifteen percent will take longer. This means at least one in six couples have problems conceiving a child.

Experiencing the inability to have a child, especially when one deeply desires one can be a deeply distressing and stressful experience. The stress can be increased by having to go through expensive treatments that have no guarantees attached.

Even though fertility is a natural thing it relies on a variety of complicated factors. God is good, but not that good cause one little glitch in the system can mean it doesn't occur or is at least delayed. That's why it's important to maintain good body balance. For 40% of the time the overall reason for fertility lies with the woman and the other 40% lies with the man.

The Dance of the Red Moon

Your Menstrual Cycle

It happens to us every month and runs up a little fortune over the course of our years in sanitary bills. Yet we know so little about "it" -   our: Monthlies, Red Moon, My Cycle.

However, getting pregnant relies on our full understanding on how our menstrual cycle works. So that we can determine when we ovulate.

To determine your ovulation day it would be a good idea to chart your "Monthlies" for at least three months. Make a note of when you first start menstruating to the day you finish. Once you know the length of your cycle just subtract fourteen from it. The number you get is the day you ovulate. So if you have a twenty eight day cycle – you will ovulate on day fourteen (28 – 14 = 14).

Once you have determined your ovulation date have sex for five days every other day up until the day of ovulation and three days afterwards. Why every other day? Too much sex may well compromise sperm count. Having intercourse daily can reduce sperm count. Also it is worth noting that Mother Nature is very clever and made sperm to survive in the Vagina for up to five days (especially if you are approaching ovulation).

The Dance of Basal Body Temperature

What on earth is that alien sounding thing? The basal body temperature (BBT) is what is known as the body's core temperature. It normally stays at 97ºF. When you ovulate your body's temperature rises slightly, going up by half a degree or a full degree to 98F or higher, and stays elevated for a number of days. Keeping track of your BBT is one of the most popular forms of natural birth control used by women today.

To chart your basal temperature you need a special thermometer known as the Basal thermometer. This can be located in any good pharmacy. Once purchased take your temperature every morning throughout your cycle. Try taking it at the same time every day, as this will allow you to identify the temperature pattern of your body. You will also be able to identify exactly when you ovulate. If you draw a line from one temperature to another it can help you to see the fluctuations in your temperature. Chart your basal temperature for several months in order to see its pattern. It's a good idea to have some fun between the sheets at least four days before you anticipate a shift in your basal body temperature and for a few days afterwards. This will increase your chances of conception.

The Dance of Mucous Monitoring

This isn't as yucky as it sounds. Our cervical mucus is actually a good fertility marker. Cervical mucus changes during the course of our monthly cycle, as it responds to the estrogen levels in our body. As we experience the first half of our cycle, the egg matures within the ovarian follicle. During this time the body releases more estrogen. This estrogen helps to thicken the lining of the uterus, preparing it for implantation of the fertilized egg. At the change of estrogen level also changes our cervical mucus making it more fertile. This fertile mucus provides an alkaline environment which allows the sperm to travel through the vagina.

After the peaking of the estrogen (at ovulation), there is a surge in the levels of progesterone. At this time the cervical mucus changes. This change can take as little as a couple of hours. During this period the opportunity for conception has passed. Fertile mucous is easy to spot. It is transparent, stringy and stretchy. If you rub it between two fingers and separate them it will stretch. Note that fertile mucus can be affected by activities like bathing, showering, and swimming.

The Dance of the Ovulation Prediction Test

An Ovulation Predictor Test kit is also a great way to predict your day of ovulation. The test detects surges in the luteinizing hormone (LH) that occurs just before ovulation. The rise of LH triggers the release of the egg from the ovary. Ovulation usually takes place twelve to thirty-six hours after the test shows as positive. A word of caution: If you are over the age of forty or approaching menopause the LH surge may not always be followed by the release of an egg. To see how accurate this way of ovulation prediction is for you try it for a few months.

The Dance of the Phallus

His Fertility

The Dance before Breakfast

Sperm counts are higher in the morning. This is generally true if you haven't made love the night before. So before breakfast get busy.

The Dance of Abstinence

It worked for me and my husband. We abstained from sex for forty days. But there are some experts that say that abstinence makes the sperm grow weaker. According to some experts regular sexual activity increases testosterone levels which stimulate sperm production and maturation. However, many traditions believe that a little abstinence goes a long way to help our vital energy system regain its balance. I think you can experiment with both ways. Or go the in between root and just abstain for just a few days at a time.

The Dance of Sexual Positions

I am afraid our parents may have been right about the good old missionary position. In order to become pregnant, it's important that your partner deposit his sperm as close as possible to your cervix. Certain positions will allow this to happen more easily than others. Avoid having sex while standing, sitting, or with you on top, as this can cause semen to leak out of your body. Instead, try the missionary position, which allows for deeper penetration. Rear entry intercourse is also effective, as it allows your partner to deposit semen closer to your cervix. To keep any extra semen from leaking out of you, try elevating your hips for fifteen minutes or so after your have sex.

The Dance of Impotence

Many men experience impotence at various stages of their existence. It can be caused by stress, fatigue, poor diet, and a physical problem. Tell your man not to be embarrassed. Seeing a professional may go a long way to help resolve the root of the issue.

Dancing the Path Notes

Attending births is like growing roses. You have to marvel at
the ones that just open up and bloom at the first kiss of the sun
but you wouldn't dream of pulling open the petals of the
tightly closed buds and forcing them to blossom to your time
line

Gloria Lemay

_____

_____

_____

_____

_____

_____

_____

_____

_____

_____

_____

_____

_____

_____

_____

_____

_____

_____

_____

_____

_____

_____

_____

_____

_____

_____

_____

_____

PART TWO

THE DANCE OF PREGNANCY: DADDY MEET BODY PILLOW:

When those two blue lines appeared on the Clear Blue stick I was so happy. My brother did light heartedly try to pop my joy of having obtained pregnancy at forty by dancing like a graceful gentle warrior through fertility. According to him back in cave man days forty was old but not anymore. So in other words achieving pregnancy at forty through infertility problems was not a big deal. I was not buying into that. I decided to remain proud of my achievements.

Little did I know those pregnancy bumps were going to try and pop all my joy, anyway. There was the morning sickness, the achy back, tired feet and headaches. Let's not talk about the weight issue. It seemed like one thing came rushing in after another.

Then I had the images of having to give birth with my legs high up in the air defying all the laws of gravity. Those images threatened to further bring down my energy.

I truly wanted to dance through my pregnancy the natural way, but every which way I turned there seemed to be someone or something to discourage the process of seeing the whole dance, as not a dance at all. The few pre-natal meetings myself and Derrick went to were real joy busters. We thought birthing was meant to be a joyful process. Oh, no. Not according to the pre-natal meetings. There were so many things that could go wrong. So many medications you were most likely to take (for your benefit of course). The pain. Yes, the pain. It was so overwhelming that you might as well take an epidural and get it over with. It's okay, if it completely numbs your legs and you can't feel a darn thing. Oh, and then you have to take more medication to counter its effects. This was the kind of advise we were given.

I remember after the first pre-natal meeting myself and Derrick went to I was beyond depressed. The thing that depressed me above everything was the idea of my legs could very likely end up being up in those dreaded stirrups (dreaded in my mind, anyway).

"In American hospitals doctors favor the stirrup position. Even though, it has been proven not to be one of the best positions to give birth in," the pre-natal instructor told the class. Who divulged going with gravity was always the best solution.

The only people who seemed perturbed at these dire birthing facts were me, Derrick and an older East Indian woman who seemed to be in her late fifties.

It was after these meetings that I confided and moaned to Derrick,

"I'm going to have a horrible birth.'

"It's going to be just fine," he would always assure.

His assurances made me feel a little better, but not much. My mood was not lifted when I had this conversation with my rather nice OB-GYN doctor.

"So doc will I be able to give birth on my knees?"

Blank stare. Deathly silence. A sweet smile.

"We try to accommodate people as much as we can."

Was it me or was I truly getting the impression that did not include me being on my knees.

I almost got lost in the tirade of joy busters, but then I stopped myself and them (the joy poppers). I decided that I would dance through my pregnancy in the way that I wanted to dance. I was not going to let anyone dictate to me how I should dance. So dance I did quite literally.

As I put the Seven Principles of Wellness into effect - what is now the Bhumi Drum Energy Dance grew with me and my bump. Everyday I danced, and danced. I grew the yoga routine in the dance more, and incorporated the self massages, aromatherapy oils, and more breath techniques.

The more I claimed my dance is the more that I glowed. More and more people began to complement me on that glow too.

As yoga, meditation, and the Seven Principles of Wellness all played a major role in my Dance of Pregnancy I want to share with you some of the facts that I discovered.

Experts say Yoga is great during the pregnancy stage. When paired with cardiovascular exercises such as walking yoga can keep us ladies in great shape during pregnancy. It also keeps us limbered, toned, improves balance and circulation. Yoga is like a moving meditation. It helps us to breathe deeply and relax. All of this comes in handy when faced with the physical demands of labor, birth and motherhood.

Pain is a funny thing. When we are in pain the natural tendency is to tighten up our whole body. That's not good for a smooth labor process. Regular yoga practice can help us to fight the urge to do this, and to relax instead.

All in all, Pre-natal yoga is really good for our physical wellbeing. It lowers blood pressure, the stress hormones, and gives that much needed emotional boast.

There's a lot of advice about do's and don'ts of Yoga during pregnancy, but I found out my body always guided me very wisely. Many Yoga experts agree with that fact. The general rule of thumb does seem to be: don't hold positions for too long; take your time and listen to your body; in your second trimester avoid lying on the floor. This position can apparently stop blood from flowing properly to the uterus.

Now in your third trimester it is advised to keep heels to the wall for standing poses. While the use of yoga blocks and straps will help aid with doing poses. If you have never done a head or shoulder stand before it is generally advised – leave them well alone. Now is not the time to be practicing these. Also the more advanced in your pregnancy you become, stay away from deep forward bends, backward bends and twist.

The benefits of meditation during pregnancy are numerous. I found meditating during my pregnancy put me right in baby bliss land. Here are some of the benefits of meditation during pregnancy which I found on www.pregnancytochildbirth.com:

1. Decreases stress.
2. Produces endorphins which reduce physical pain.
3. Increases production of DHEA (dehydroepiandrosterone), which stimulates the

production of T and B lymphocytes, thus supporting the immune system. DHEA also makes you feel better and enhances brain biochemistry, preventing sadness and depression before and after birth.

4. Decreases the production of adrenalin and cortisol

5. Increases the levels of melatonin, thus supporting the immune system, increasing the quality of sleep, and improving moods.

6. Increases the production of endorphins, which have a very strong pain-relieving effect in preparation for childbirth. The more time devoted to the practice of prenatal meditation the higher the level of endorphins at birth. Endorphin production is important to a woman in avoiding the risks of medical intervention.

7. Prevents pre-eclampsia. Meditation can be very effective in lowering blood pressure and heart rate, lowering the risk of pre-eclampsia and potential preterm brain damage.

8. Eliminates negative emotions, which if prolonged can affect your baby's development in uterus.

9. Releases fear of labor by empowering you through the process of childbirth. You learn that each contraction is the biological way your baby communicates with you to tell you when he or she is coming. Facing each contraction with the power of deep relaxation and not with fear is the key to achieving natural childbirth.

10. Increases milk production, and prevents postpartum depression. It is important to learn how to be present, be in the moment and love yourself and your baby unconditionally.

I would also add that you can use meditation as a time to visualize a positive joyful birth. The exercise below is a simple one you can use to do so:

Womb Breathing Exercise

Lie down in a quiet space. Use your inhalation and exhalation to take you into a place of deep relaxation. When you feel sufficiently relaxed imagine yourself walking down a flight of ten steps into your womb. As you do so count from ten to zero. By the time you reach zero you should be in your womb area. Make yourself cozy there and visualize exactly how you would like your pregnancy and birthing to go. You can use this Womb Breathing exercise to visualize and recreate any situation in your life. For the womb is the place where all things that are to be birthed grow.

The Dance of Remedies

Now I want to share with you, because I want you to dance to, the remedies that I discovered to get me through some common pregnancy symptoms.

The Dance of Morning Sickness

My first hurdle to overcome was the dreaded morning sickness. I was lucky. I didn't have it with my first pregnancy. No such luck the second time round. I joined the morning sickness club. In other words I joined the fifty percent of my pregnant sisters. According to experts morning sickness starts around the sixth week of pregnancy. It normally affects more than half of all pregnant women and is meant to get worse with each successive pregnancy. It is the nauseated feeling you get during pregnancy which can be accompanied by vomiting. They say the nausea is often a result of the increased hormones in your body.

I asked my doctor what to do about it. They kindly offered me medication and I kindly refused. It was my first pregnancy ailment and I did not intend to go down that rocky rood. So what did I do as an alternative? Well, I knew that Chamomile had always worked in the past to settle my queasy stomachs. I also knew it was a calmative. I concluded it would therefore be good for my morning sickness. I did a little more research from my favorite herbalist David Hoffman and found this to be the case. So I got drinking two cups a day and bingo – reduced morning sickness. It was fab, because that morning sickness stuff is no joke.

Just a few facts on chamomile. German or wild chamomile grows to 2ft/60 cm in height and has feathery aromatic flowers. The name Chamomile comes from the Greek word Kamai melon which means "ground apple," because the herb grows at soil level and has an apple-like aroma. The plant is known as the "plant physician" because it promotes a healthy garden. The flowers of the plant are used and they contain an essential oil.

Other important ingredients in the flowers and leaves are healing flavonoids, fatty acids, amino acids, bitters, and tannin; the properties are anti-inflammatory, antispasmodic and sedative. As a herbal infusion or oil chamomile can be used to help with other conditions besides morning sickness such as helping soothe skin irritations. When its fresh or dried flowers are infused they help ease indigestion of the nervous origin, insomnia, mood swings and irritability. It soothes the membranes of the digestive tract.

It is said that the Egyptians dedicated Chamomile to their sun god and valued it over all other herbs for its healing qualities. Due to its sedative and relaxing properties Chamomile was an ingredient in some love potions in the middle ages.

Morning Sickness Be Gone Tea

Ingredients
2 teaspoons Fresh Chamomile Flowers
Directions
*Put all ingredients in a small saucepan filled with
water*
Simmer for five minutes
Strain
Stir in milk
Sweeten with a little bit of honey
Drink twice to three times a day
Store excess in fridge

Dancing With Fatigue

So I had just got over the hurdle of morning sickness. Then came tiredness. I was adamant it was not going to win the battle. So I got my sword out and prepared to do battle. I made a phone call to my herbalist in London and researched my little heart out. I stuck my head out from the trenches and came up with a battery of things that really worked. There were two things in particular that made me feel an almost instant victory: the herbs of Nettle and Yellow Dock, along with the traditional Indian Foot Massage

Before you go rushing off to buy up your natural food store supply, take note. I discovered that it is normal to feel fatigued during the first trimester as pregnancy puts a strain on the entire body. Even night owls will struggle with staying awake. It is possible that hormonal changes, particularly a dramatic rise in progesterone contribute to that feeling of tiredness that swamps us. Tiredness can also be caused by not being able to get a good night's sleep, anxiety, nausea and vomiting which can all tax our energy. By the second trimester most of us feel like our old selves again, only most probably to lose steam by the seventh trimester.

Tiredness may also be a sign of anemia so it is worth telling the doctor about your symptoms. Preventing anemia is a very important part of ante-natal care. Hemoglobin, the iron and protein compound contained in red blood cells (erythrocytes), is responsible for transporting oxygen from the lungs around the body including (of course) both placenta and fetus.

If hemoglobin levels in the blood fall, so too does the body's ability to access oxygen. Anemia can be identified by the following symptoms: lethargy, irritability, breathlessness on slight exertion. It can occur at any time in pregnancy especially because the baby is taking up higher proportions of the mother's iron. It is a good idea to build up iron reserves before pregnancy starts so that you can meet the increased iron demands without any problems.

My feelings of tiredness were caused by general pregnancy stress and strains, and definitely by anemia.

The Herbal Remedy

Back to Nettles and Yellow Dock. It is interesting that nettles are often regarded as a troublesome weed however they are one of the most invaluable medicinal and horticultural plants. Once used by Roman Soldiers who use to rub the plant on their skin to relieve cold and damp Nettles are widely used for their astringent properties. They have an all around tonic, anti-rheumatic and blood purifying effects. They are packed with Formic acid, tannins, histamine, chlorophyll, minerals (iron, potassium, manganese, and sulfur); as well as vitamins A and C. Besides helping you feel better during your pregnancy Nettles are used to great effect in some cases of rheumatism, arthritis, and childhood eczema. As an astringent they may be used for nose bleeds or to relieve the symptoms wherever there is hemorrhage in the body, for example in uterine hemorrhage.

Yellow Dock has quite a bitter taste, but it is a wonderful herb. I know, because before pregnancy I lived by it. It is packed with goodness. Its active ingredients are Anthraquinone glocosides (about 3-4%). It also contains healthy compounds such as nepodin, tannins, rumicin, oxalates, and has high levels of iron. It is an alterative, laxative, hepatic, cholagogue, and good overall tonic. It is used in helping to support the relief of fatigue in pregnancy, chronic skin complaints, constipation. While promoting the good flow of bile, acting as an excellent and gentle blood cleanser, and helps treatment for jaundice. It is said that Yellow Dock was used by Native American Indians to treat boils. It was also claimed the concoction was used traditionally to draw money, business customers and love.

The Traditional Foot Massage

Bliss, Bliss, Bliss is the Indian Foot massage. Even though I had been using this massage for years. It took on a whole new meaning during my pregnancy journey. Not only did it soothe my achy swollen feet, it lifted my mood and re-energized my whole mind-body and soul.

The first image of the blissful foot massage can be spotted in an Egyptian picture which dates back 2500 BC. It shows Egyptian doctors massaging the feet of patients. From Egypt the foot massage seemed to travel onto Greece, India, China and Japan. There is much information about the foot massage in the Internal Classic of the Yellow Emperor (475 – 221 BC).

The feet have 7,300 nerve endings. The East Indian and Chinese classical medical text showed that there are over 600 pressure points in the body. 66 of them are in the feet. They link directly to vital organs in the body. The foot massage may have travelled from Egypt. However in the West the scientific basis of reflexology has its roots in early neurological studies conducted in the 1890's by Sir Henry Head, of England. He established "Head zones" and conclusively proved the neurological relationship existing between the skin and the internal organs.

It was Connecticut physician, William Fitzgerald who discovered he could prevent pain in minor surgery by pressing pressure points in the hand. He identified "reflex zones" of the body and called his work "zone therapy". He discovered ten zones run vertically from the top of your head down to the soles of the feet. Five on the right and five on the left with each zone ending at one of your toes. Every organ, gland or bodily structure is located within one of these zones.

Thereafter, it was the American nurse and Physical therapist, Eunice D, who was highly intuitive and spent 40 years charting the effects of the reflex zones in the feet. She created the first maps showing exactly where to press. This is when "Reflex Zone Therapy" became renamed as reflexology.

Ancient Egyptian Foot Massage.

Supplements

Taking Iron supplements really did help to remedy this condition too. Check with your doctor to see if you are anemic. If you are they will recommend iron. Even if you are not it is good to keep up with your iron intake.

Enhancing the Foot Massage

I found the Indian foot massage was definitely good at helping to remedy many of my pregnancy issues such as: constipation, fatigue, headaches, sleeplessness etc. This was especially true when I pressed and massaged certain points. So it is worth familiarizing yourself with a Reflexology map of the feet and knowing which parts of the feet correspond to which organs of the body. Then during your Indian foot massage just press the appropriate point when needed.

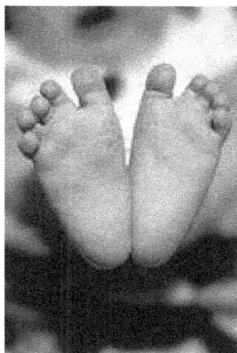

Foot Reflexology

1. Brain: top of toes
2. Ears/Eyes/Sinuses: Fleshy part of toes
3. Neck/Helper to Eyes and Ears: base of toes
4. Chest or Lungs: Middle of upper foot
5. Solar Plexus: Center of foot
6. Colon: Towards edge of outer foot
7. Spine: Inner edge of foot

Traditional Indian Foot Massage

Need

Base Oil (Olive, Soy, Almond or Sunflower)

Directions

- Rub a small amount of oil into feet.
- Imagine your feet has five lines running from the heel all the way to the top of your toes. These are actually the energy lines of the feet which correspond to the energy channels of the whole body.
- Using a sweeping motion massage along these lines in sequence. Start from the inside line to the outside line. Work your way from the heel of the foot right to the top of the toes. Do this sequence for twenty times.
- Next massage the middle of your feet in a circular motion. This area corresponds to the solar plexus, and the stomach. Massaging it helps circulate energy throughout your whole system.
- Now do twenty more rounds of sweeping strokes.

Fatigue Relief Tea

Ingredients

2 teaspoons Nettle herb

2 teaspoons Yellow Dock herb

Directions

Put all ingredients in a small saucepan filled with water

Simmer for fifteen minutes

Strain

Dancing With Constipation

Constipation. All who want to talk about it put your hands up? If it was a normal classroom, all hands would definitely be down. Us ladies in the pregnancy club however eagerly put our hands up. Cause constipation is a really real issue for us. Anyway, it was for me. They tell you nothing is worse than a hungry man. Well just try a constipated pregnant woman's temper!

What's up with the whole poop thing? Why does the darn thing get so hard when you're pregnant? (Pardon the pun). Apparently progesterone relaxes the intestinal muscles reducing their power to expel our poop. Then there is the weight of the baby and the increase of the placenta. With the progression of pregnancy they both exert pressure on the lower bowel aggravating constipation. The enlargement of the uterus also impedes circulation to the bowel restricting the action of the intestinal muscle. Also, tension or anxiety, the intake of iron supplements, eating small starchy meals consisting of refined flour also contribute to the problem.

What's the secret to relieving constipation during pregnancy? I discovered that a tea made of Yellow Dock, Dandelion and Aniseed are useful. I have already spoken in detail about the properties of Yellow Dock. What about Dandelion and Aniseed?

Dandelion was used in Ancient Greek times as a cleansing and diuretic medicine. In Britain the leaves were used to make a beer known as "Dandelion and Burdock". The leaves and roots of dandelion like most herbs are packed with goodness. They contain bitters, sterols, tannin, glycosides, resin, essential oil, high levels of potassium, vitamins A and C. All this makes Dandelion an excellent support for the liver, digestive stimulant, diuretic and overall tonic.

Dandelion also is used to great effect in cases of water retention due to heart problems, inflammation and congestion of liver and gall bladder, chronic jaundice, auto-intoxication, rheumatism, blood disorders, chronic skin eruptions, chronic gastritis and ulcers.

Aniseed not only tastes delicious but is also packed with all the natural goodness of nature. It is a Expectorant, anti-spasmodic, carminative, anti-microbial, aromatic, galactagogue. The volatile oil in Aniseed provides the basis for its internal use to ease griping, intestinal colic and flatulence. It also has an expectorant and anti-spasmodic action and may be used in bronchitis, in tracheitis where there is persistent irritable coughing, and in whooping cough.

Aniseed has been demonstrated to increase mucociliary transport and so supporting its use as an expectorant. It has mild estrogenic effects, thought to be due to the presence of dianethole and photoanethole, which explains the use of this plant in folk medicine to increase milk secretion, facilitate birth and increase libido. Aniseed is also good for treating skin problems like scabies.

Poop Relief Tea

Ingredients

2 teaspoons Dandelion root

2 teaspoons Aniseed

2 teaspoons Yellow Dock Root

Directions

Put all ingredients in a small saucepan filled with water, simmer, strain and sip at least two cups a day.

Dancing With an Infection Down There

I was burning, stinging and urinating a lot. It soon became obvious that I had a urinary infection. It was a puzzling affair as I knew Derrick was defiantly not the root cause (just wanted to get that one out of your head!). Then what was the problem? My OB-GYN doctor soon let me on to a secret – lots of women get vaginal infections during pregnancy.

"It's due to the changes in the vagina during pregnancy," he said smiling.

I did some more research and found out it was true. What was the remedy then? Antibiotics? It was the one time that I did take medication during my pregnancy. I really didn't want to but I had read enough to realize that infections could cause serious problems with the fetus. My doctor assured me that the antibiotics were safe to take. I did not feel that trustful of those little pills, but I popped them anyway. All the time I kept on quietly worrying that I was harming the baby, but I can tell you that Omo is bright, alert and beautiful.

The infection cleared up very quickly. I also brewed and drank Corn Silk and Marshmallow tea. Marshmallow is very effective in helping to calm down inflammation of the internal tissues. Corn Silk is a gentle yet powerful diuretic and urinary tract healer. It takes away the burning, stingy and painful feeling on urination we get when we have a vaginal infection.

Infection Relief Tea

Ingredients
Teaspoons of Marshmallow
2 teaspoons of Cornsilk
Directions
Put in a small saucepan filled with water
Simmer for fifteen minutes
Strain
Sip

Dancing With Headaches and Anxiety

Nothing hurts like your head pounding. Mine did in the early and middle parts of my pregnancy. In fact I experienced headaches on and off throughout the whole of my pregnancy. For many, headaches in pregnancy occur during their first and third trimesters. They are caused by a surge in hormones. Experiencing headaches during pregnancy is one of the most common discomforts and complaints.

Headaches may occur at any time during your pregnancy, but they tend to be most common during the first and third trimesters. An increase in headaches during the first trimester is believed to be caused by the surge of hormones along with an increase in the blood volume circulating throughout your body. These headaches may be further aggravated by stress, poor posture, sinuses or changes in your vision. Other causes of headaches during pregnancy may involve one or more of the following: Lack of sleep, low blood sugar, dehydration and caffeine withdrawal. During the third trimester headaches may be related to tension from carrying heavy things, poor posture or preeclampsia (high blood pressure during pregnancy).

I found that my headaches were helped by getting lots of rest and relaxation, gentle exercise and making sure I was eating well. It is also suggested that one checks posture as poor posture can also be a culprit. For a sinus headache it is a good idea to apply a warm compress around your eyes and nose; while a tension headache is helped by a cold compress or ice pack at the base of your neck. Massage also alleviates headaches, especially a good massage to the shoulders and neck. "Hubby, where are you?!"

Brewing and drinking Chamomile tea during the day also helped with alleviating my headaches as it is a calmative. Adding Valerian and Skullcap to the tea helps to alleviate stress and headaches. We know quite a bit about Chamomile by now, but what about Valerian and Skullcap?

In Ancient Greek times Valerian was known as "Phu" which referred to its strong odor. During medieval times it was known as "All Heal". It is an excellent nervine and relaxant along with Skullcap which also relaxes nervous tension while tonifying and renewing the nervous system. It is also very good for the treatment of seizures, hysterical states, epilepsy, depression and pre-menstrual tension. Skullcap is perhaps the most widely relevant nervine available to us in the world of herbal medicine.

Headache & Anxiety Relief Tea

Ingredients
2 teaspoons of Chamomile flowers
1 teaspoon of valerian
1 teaspoon of Comfrey

Directions
Put all ingredients in a small saucepan filled with water
Simmer for fifteen minutes
Strain
Stir in milk
Sweeten with a little bit of honey
Drink twice a day
Store excess in fridge

Dancing With the Heartburn

I did not suffer from Heartburn during my pregnancy but its worth mentioning it here because many women do. In fact, it is apparently another one of those common complaints us ladies have during pregnancy.

It is caused by the reflux of gastric contents into the esophagus due to back pressure. The relaxing effects of progesterone reach the cardiac sphincter and the valve guarding the entrance to the stomach at the bottom of the esophagus. As a result of this, the enlarging uterus pushes up against the stomach; small amounts of the stomach's contents are passed into the lower esophagus. Hydrochloric acid mixed with the stomach contents irritate and burn the esophagus, and result in an inflammatory process. In more extreme cases, parts of the stomach itself can be pushed up through the diaphragm or into the esophagus, and cause some degree of hiatus hernia. Your symptoms of heartburn can be eased by doing some of the following:

- *Avoid food and beverages that cause you gastrointestinal distress.* The usual suspects are carbonated drinks; alcohol (which you should avoid anyway during pregnancy); caffeine; chocolate; acidic foods like citrus fruits and juices, tomatoes, mustard, and vinegar; processed meats; mint products; and spicy, highly seasoned, fried, or fatty foods
- *Don't eat big meals.* Instead, eat several small meals throughout the day. Take your time eating and chew

thoroughly

- *Avoid drinking large quantities of fluids during meals* — you don't want to distend your stomach. (It's important to drink eight to ten glasses of water daily during pregnancy, but sip it between meals.)
- *Try chewing gum after eating.* Chewing gum stimulates your salivary glands, and saliva can help neutralize acid.
- *Don't eat close to bedtime.* Give yourself two to three hours to digest before you lie down.
- *Sleep propped up with several pillows or a wedge.* Elevating your upper body will help keep your stomach acids where they belong and will aid your digestion.
- *Gain a sensible amount of weight,* and stay within the guidelines your healthcare provider suggests.
- *Wear loose, comfortable clothing.* Avoid any tightness around your waist and tummy.
- *Bend at the knees* instead of at the waist.
- *Don't smoke* — in addition to contributing to a host of serious health problems, smoking boosts stomach acidity. (Ideally, smoking is a habit you should break before getting pregnant. If you're still smoking and are having trouble quitting, ask your caregiver for a referral to a smoking-cessation program.)

A good tea to drink is a combination of one that is calming, soothing, anti-inflammatory, and helps to clean the blood. One such tea consists of Calendula, Chamomile, Marshmallow and Comfrey. We have already spoken about the super qualities of my favorite herb for pregnancy, Chamomile. However, what about the others mentioned in this tea.

Calendula like chamomile has beautiful fragrant yellow flowers that are used to brew healing teas. My son saw some Calendula tea I boiled just a few days ago and said "mommy I didn't know you can drink sunflower tea". I looked at the tea and thought "that's interesting the flowers really do look a little like sunflowers once they have been brewed."

Calendula is a delightful herb and I love it for its gentle yet powerful healing properties. It is anti-inflammatory, cleansing, diuretic, a good blood cleanser, lymphatic and astringent. It is renowned as a skin healer, for cleansing wounds and promoting tissue repair. It is also great in soothing the digestive tract. In an old 18th century herbal it is listed as good for strengthening the heart, toothache, headaches and jaundice.

Marshmallow's root and leaf are used for herbal decoctions. It is a gentle but powerful demulcent, emollient, diuretic, anti-inflammatory, expectorant. It has an abundance of mucilage which makes it an excellent demulcent. The roots are often used for aiding in healing of the digestive system while the leaves are used more for the urinary and lung systems. Conditions such as gastritis, peptic ulcerations, colitis, cystitis, urinary gravel, bronchitis, respiratory catarrhs and coughs are helped with the help of Marshmallow. When used as an ointment it can go a long way in aiding in the treatment of inflamed wounds, burns & scalds, bedsores and boils.

Comfrey's name comes from the Greek *sympho* which means "combined together" and *vhyto* which means plant. It is also called by the name of Knit Bones. This is all very befitting of this herb which my husband loves and swears by. For Comfrey has a long and established history as a potent skin and bone healer. It is a vulnerary, demulcent, anti-inflammatory, astringent, and expectorant. Its soothing demulcent and anti-inflammatory qualities is what will help you with your heartburn issues.

Heartburn Relief Tea

Ingredients
2 teaspoons of fresh Calendula flowers
2 teaspoons of Chamomile flowers
1 teaspoons of Marshmallow
1 teaspoons of Comfrey

Directions
Put all ingredients in a small saucepan filled with water
Simmer for fifteen minutes
Strain
Stir in milk
Sweeten with a little bit of honey
Drink twice a day

Dancing With the ZZZZs

Tell your husbands and boyfriends that the body pillow will not replace him. He will buy it for you out of kindness and be sure to whine about it once it is in your life. The problem is once it is in your life it won't leave. Six months after giving birth, I still use mine. Honestly, it doesn't replace Derrick. Well............ Come on admit it – those body pillows are so darn comfortable. Especially, in pregnancy when you just can't get that sweet spot for resting

A National Sleep Foundation poll found that over three-quarters of women slept worse during pregnancy than they did when they weren't pregnant. What's more, new moms and pregnant women were more likely to suffer insomnia than any other group of women. The reason? Simple, that little bundle of joy is growing and moving inside.

How you sleep is important in helping you get those all-important zzzz's. Conventional wisdom sates you may have to adjust your sleeping habits so that you sleep on your side. Some experts say that lying flat on your back may not be the way to go.

"There's some concern about that in the latter part of pregnancy," says Richard Henderson, MD, an obstetrician/gynecologist at St. Francis Hospital in Wilmington, Del.

When you lie on your back, the weight of the pregnant uterus slows the return of blood to your heart, which reduces blood flow to the fetus. That means the baby is getting less oxygen and fewer nutrients.

Now back to the dreaded body pillow. Tell hubby or boyfriend that the experts really do recommend it. Besides the body pillow I had another secret to gaining that much needed sleep – it came in the form of Derrick and a bottle of my Chamomile Body Rub Oil (see the simple version below). When Derrick rubbed my stomach or massaged my back with it, he said it made him feel close to me and the baby. In fact, the oil often sent him to sleep too!

Then there's the chamomile tea from the *Morning Sickness* section. That worked a treat too.

Chamomile Oil Rub

Ingredients
10 drops of Chamomile
Sunflower or oil of your choosing

Directions
Mix the Chamomile essential oil and base oil of your choosing. Bottle in bottle of choice. Now Shake and get rubbing!

Dancing with the Weight

Went and had my pre-natal checkup. This one was really quick. The baby's heart beat is still strong. Still amazed at how fast it sounds. Since the pregnancy I have put on almost 40 pounds in weight. I am wondering if most of that weight is due to the pregnancy or due to me over eating while I have been pregnant. I am suspecting a little of the former and much of the latter. I won't lie my weight gain is getting me down. I am 21 weeks and I feel like an elephant. I'm so conscious of my weight gain that I did pick up Weight Watchers magazine. I have only read it once in my life. While reading it, it did dawn on me I don't have to focus on weight loss but on eating a little bit (okay much) less. I can cut down on the gauging. Oh, and buying a new bra one size up (which was still too small) did not make me feel any better. You would think I would be happy to go from a 34B to a 34D. I thought so too. At first when my little oranges were growing I was like, 'Oh cool!'. Now I enviously look at the 34B Bras thinking how cute they look.

Okay, so were pregnant and we are not meant to talk about weight. It's good, it's healthy and it's part of pregnancy. We are glowing Earth Mothers (Is that a compliment or a back handed way of saying "you're getting fat?!"). Talking about weight and pregnancy seems to be like trying to find the Holy Grail. You just don't do it. So instead we secrete our thoughts in our minds, the next doughnut and of course our diaries. A bit like I did (proof above. That by the way was my journal entrance for April 21st 2010).

I am owning up - weight was quite an issue for me early on in my pregnancy. I was obsessing about my weight often. It's not that I wasn't excited about being pregnant, especially after so many years of being infertile. However, that did not stop me trying to cling on to my slim self. I bought beautiful big flowy tops and dresses. Yes, because they were the most comfortable things to wear. Also, because I thought they made me look elegantly slim.

That was until one day we went to Myrtle Beach to celebrate my 40th birthday and the hotel front of desk man said,

"Ma'am, be careful with all the walking you intend to do."

"Why?" I asked politely and quite puzzled.

"You know being so pregnant. It might not be that safe."

"How did he know I was pregnant?" I asked Derrick latter that day. "The man must be a genius."

"Sweetie, are you serious? Your stomach is sticking out for the whole world to see!"

"No it's not!" I retorted.

"Yes, it is. Just look at this picture on the camera if you don't believe me."

He switched on our little silver digital camera and went to pictures my son had taken of me at an animal conservation place. I was horribly shocked. I had on my lovely yellow flowy dress. To my disappointment

I looked not like a slim gym (as we say in London), but like that wonderful glowing Earth Mother.

"Oh hell!" I paused and finished the sentence "well, I don't think I look pregnant."

"Nah, sweetie you don't look pregnant at seven months," Derrick smiled. Giving me a manly hug and sweet kiss on the forehead.

Let's talk about the cravings. I started having them in the early stages of my pregnancy. It started with Chinese food. That lasted a few months until the waitress started showing way too much of an interest in my husband! After that I switched to a weekly ice cream craving.

Then there was the constant eating. Something I reinforced with the mantra "you are eating for two. You are eating for two." It was one that worked until my Ob/Gyn weekly appointments revealed that I was putting on 10 lbs. or more a week. They reassured me that a little weight gain a week was normal. But deep down I knew that some of my weight gain was due to some serious over indulgence. Even though everyone constantly told me to make sure I ate a lot for my nutritional requirements I had the lurking suspicion that too much weight gain was unhealthy. I also remembered my Ayurvedic training taught me that eating a lot did not mean we were meeting our nutritional needs. There was more to it than that. What and how we ate were also crucial considerations.

Then I picked up my copy of *Healthy Mom & Baby* which had a timely article called "Healthy Weight Gain" by Carolyn M. Clancy, MD. The article claimed recent studies demonstrated there is "a great risk associated with gaining too little weight during pregnancy. There's also a great risk in gaining too much weight." But what is too much and too little weight gain? The article addressed this through a BMI (Body Mass Index) chart. You will find a BMI chart on the next page.

Once I owned up to my binging excuses I immediately sought to put in *The Seven Principles of Wellness* into action. I also remembered a little trick to getting lots of nutrients without putting on weight – juicing. I knew about the benefits of juicing from my old days of juicing. It is surprising to me that I have not spied the benefits of juicing in any of the pregnancy magazines. Mind you, that's not to say they have never covered the topic.

Juicing is also a very powerful method of ensuring our cells, tissues, and organs receive instant nourishment. This is something I recommend that we all add into our daily diets. The uplifting and rejuvenating power of juice is truly miraculous. With natural juice, the digestive system gets a chance to rest but receive all the nourishment it needs. This is important as many of us are eating but due to the impairment of the digestive system we are unable to absorb all the nutrients we need from our food.

Juicing also provides us with an abundance of fresh enzymes which are necessary for all bio-chemical activity in the body. In one glass of juice you can eat 2 apples, 4 carrots, ¼ beetroot, spinach and ginger. You can also do this several times a day!

When I started juicing I noticed my skin was glowing, my energy levels were up, creative powers flowing, hunger levels were down (a craving for food is due to nutrients missing from the body particularly micronutrients), I was calmer, my bowel movements were better and I was not waking up as sluggish in the mornings.

Needless to say, armed with a new attitude and nutritional principles I stopped looking so anxiously at every Weight Watchers magazine I came across! Check out the juicing and healthy nutritional principles and tips in the first section of the book. Also a good book on juicing wouldn't go amiss.

Oh, there is one golden secret I would like to share with you. If you don't want to pile on the weight during pregnancy and post pregnancy do invest in gluten free bread, pasta etc. You can eat gluten free bread to your hearts content.

On a final note, I would like to add that while we ensure our weight is healthy so we can have a healthy pregnancy, and baby – let's not forget we are indeed glowing beautiful Earth Mothers. For we begin to replicate Mother Earth physically, emotionally and spiritually. Her cycles and rhythms begin to sync at one with ours. That is a beautiful thing – to hold her energy and the growing life force within ourselves.

Pregnancy BMI Chart

Your BMI	Appropriate Weight Gain During Pregnancy
19.7 or lower	28.40 pounds
19.8 to 26	25 to 35 pounds
26.1 to 29	15 to 25 pounds
29.1 or higher	At least 15 pounds

If you want to find out your BMI go to health4mom.org/calculator. Also remember the chart is just a guide. We are all very different people

Yes & No Foods for Pregnancy

Yes Foods
Fruits
Vegetables
Fish (especially salmon and trout)
Lean poultry (non fried)
Legumes
Nuts
Dried beans and peas
Cereal grains
Low-fat dairy or dairy substitutes

No Foods
Saturated and trans fats
Simple sugars
Syrups

Dancing With Pregnancy – Some More Facts

Yoga Moves for Labor

As my pregnancy advanced, Derrick suggested that I find yoga positions that would aid in labor. So I did some research and here are some positions I found and tried out. What I found was not all the positions suggested sat comfortably with my body (yours will to). That was okay. I just discarded them. As I said, my body always seemed to know best! My favorite pose was the warrior pose. In Sanskrit, that is an old sacred language of India, this pose is called Tadasana. It is the name of a fierce warrior incarnation of Shiva, described as having a thousand heads, a thousand eyes, and a thousand feet. He wields a thousand clubs, and wears a tiger's skin. See the next page for instructions on the warrior pose which are adapted from the Yoga Journal website. The other positions and instructions I found and adjusted from www.babycenter.com.

The Warrior Pose

- Stand in Tadasana. With an exhalation, step or lightly jump your feet 3 1/2 to 4 feet apart. Raise your arms parallel to the floor and reach them actively out to the sides, shoulder blades wide, palms down.

- Turn your right foot in slightly to the right and your left foot out to the left 90 degrees. Align the left heel with the right heel. Firm your thighs and turn your left thigh outward so that the center of the left knee cap is in line with the center of the left ankle.

- Exhale and bend your left knee over the left ankle, so that the shin is perpendicular to the floor. If possible, bring the left thigh parallel to the floor. Anchor this movement of the left knee by strengthening the right leg and pressing the outer right heel firmly to the floor.

- Stretch the arms away from the space between the shoulder blades, parallel to the floor. Don't lean the torso over the left thigh: Keep the sides of the torso equally long and the shoulders directly over the pelvis. Press the tailbone slightly toward the pubis. Turn the head to the left and look out over the fingers.

- Stay for 30 seconds to 1 minute. Inhale to come up. Reverse the feet and repeat for the same length of time to the left.

Cobbler's or Tailor's pose *(*baddha konasana)

This sitting pose helps open the pelvis. If you are very loose-jointed in your hips, make sure your "sit bones" are well grounded on the mat or blanket (gently pulling the flesh on each side of your bottom out a bit will help you find the right position). Place pillows or rolled-up towels under your knees to avoid hyperextension of your hips.

- Sit up straight against a wall with the soles of your feet touching each other.
- Gently press your knees down and away from each other, but don't force them apart.
- Stay in this position for as long as you're comfortable.

Pelvic tilt or Cat-Cow

This position helps relieve back pain, a common problem during pregnancy.

- Get on your hands and knees, arms shoulder-width apart and knees hip-width apart, keeping your arms straight, but not locking the elbows.
- Tuck your buttocks under and round your back as you breathe in.
- Relax your back into a neutral position as you breathe out.
- Repeat at your own pace.

Squatting

Squat every day to relax and open the pelvis and strengthen the upper legs. As you start to feel heavier in pregnancy, use props such as yoga blocks or a few stacked books on which to rest your bottom. Focus on relaxing and letting your breath drop deeply into your belly.

- Stand facing the back of a chair with your feet slightly wider than hip-width apart, toes pointed outward. Hold the back of the chair for support.
- Contract your abdominal muscles, lift your chest, and relax your shoulders. Then lower your tailbone toward the floor as though you were going to sit down on a chair. Find your balance — most of your weight should be toward your heels.
- Take a deep breath and, exhaling, push into your legs to rise to a standing position.

The Path of Pampering for Earth Mothers

I believe that natural remedies for our pregnancy dance do not have to be medicinal feeling or tasting. They can be a source of great delight and pampering while tackling our issues of stress, and need to feel special. It is my pleasure to share some remedies that help you dance like the beautiful Earth Mother that you are. All ingredients can be purchased from your local health food store.

Simple Goddess Sea Bath

For the ultimate in relaxation and ease on the budget

Ingredients
2 cups of Sea Salt
2 cups of Epsom Salt

Directions
Add all ingredients to bath
Soak for 15 to 20 minutes

Chamomile Goddess Bath

This bath is very calming and helps to de-stress tired achy muscles.

Ingredients
2 cups of Sea Salt
2 cups of Epsom Salt
5 cups of Chamomile herbal infusion

Directions
Add all ingredients to bath
Soak for 15 to 20 minutes

Ylang Ylang Goddess Bath

Ylang Ylang is renowned for its heavenly
aphrodisiac scent and properties.

Ingredients
2 cups of Sea Salt
2 cups of Epsom Salt
5 cups of Chamomile herbal infusion
10 drops of Ylang Ylang

Directions
Add all Ingredients to bath
Soak for 15 to 20 minutes

Goddess Orange Milk Bath

Orange is oh so yummy, and milk is the symbol
of the Goddess

Ingredients
2 cups of Sea Salt
2 cups of Epsom Salt
5 cups of Chamomile herbal infusion
10 drops of Orange essential oil
1 cup of Almond/Rice milk

Directions
Add all ingredients to bath
Soak for 15 to 20 minutes

Goddess Bubbly Fruit Bath

Nothing's as sweet as Tangerine and bubbles.

Ingredients
2 cups of Sea Salt
2 cups of Epsom Salt
10 drops of Tangerine Oil
¼ cup of unscented hypo allergenic bubble bath

Directions
Mix all ingredients in a container

Add to bath

Caribbean Goddess Bath Oil

Mix this skin lubricating and intoxicating Island scented bath oil in a small bottle. When ready add a few tea spoons to your bath.

Ingredients

1 cup base of oil (try olive, soy or almond)

10 drops of Tangerine Oil

10 drops of Ylang Ylang Oil

5 drops of Ginger Oil

2 cups of Epsom Salt

Directions

Mix all ingredients in a small bottle

Add a few teaspoons of bath mixture and Epsom salt to your bath

Soak for 15 to 20 minutes

Goddess Facial Steam Bath

Ahhhhh.

Ingredients

1 cup of Calendula infusion

5 drops of Chamomile

Directions

Put all ingredients in a bowl of hot water

Steam face for 10 for 15 minutes

Orange & Ginger Goddess Scrub

Use this delicious scrub for body or feet.

Ingredients
1-1/2 cups fine brown sugar
8 drops ginger and orange oil
1/4 cup jojoba oil and/olive oil
1/4 cup liquid unscented soap

Directions
Place sugar into a large bowl and stir to break up
any clumps. Add the essential oils, then the jojoba
oil and liquid unscented soap. Mix well and then
pour into a clean container.
To use, stand in the tub or shower and massage
the sugar scrub onto your skin from head to toe.
Rinse.

Goddess Chamomile & Honey Scrub

This delicious non oily scrub is exotically moisturizing and calming all at the same time. Use for the body or feet.

Ingredients
1 cup fine loose salt or loose sugar
3 teaspoons liquid glycerin
1 teaspoon pure honey
3-5 drops of your favorite Chamomile or your favorite essential oil.

Directions
Mix ingredients together and store in an airtight container. Add more liquid ingredients if you prefer a thinner end-product. Stir thoroughly before use.
This keeps very well, and in fact, the honey acts as preservative
Gently scrub body from head to toe

Simple Goddess Scrub

If you have no other ingredients but Sea Salt and some oil you can make this simple effective scrub which will invigorate your whole system. Use for the body or feet.

Ingredients
1 cup fine loose Sea Salt
3 to 4 teaspoons of oil (olive, almond, or soy oil)

Directions
Mix ingredients well and store in an airtight container. Add more liquid ingredients if you prefer a thinner end-product. Stir thoroughly before use. Gently scrub from head to toe.

Goddess Velvet Face & Body Oil

Ingredients
1 cup of oil (sunflower, soya, olive or almond)
1 teaspoon of Vitamin E
A few drops of Glycerin

Optional
Add choice of essential oil

Directions
Pour into bottle, shake and massage into body
daily.

Goddess Sooth My Feet Oil

This did the trick for my Goddess Tootsies!

Ingredients
1 cup of oil (Soy, Olive, Almond or Sunflower)
1 teaspoon of Vitamin E
Just a few drops of glycerin
10 drops of chamomile
10 drops of Ylang Ylang or Tangerine

Directions
Put all ingredients into bottle of choice, shake and massage into feet when needed.

Adonis Body Oil

One for the men. They deserve a massage too!

One to de-stress our honeys.

Ingredients

Bath Oil

1 cup oil (try olive, soy or almond)

10 drops of Tangerine Oil

10 drops of Ylang Ylang Oil

5 drops of Ginger Oil

10 drops of Chamomile Oil

The Dance of Dreams

So many times I have seen the pregnancy dreams put down to pure psychology. You know things we are trying to work out. But when we are pregnant I believe that the dreams we have are highly significant. In the Island Caribbean culture that I am from pregnancy dreams are paid close attention to. We believe, and know from experience that they hold much information about the child's appearance, future, and many many messages that seem to be passed onto us from the land of angels, guides, and the spirit of the baby themselves.

A year before I was pregnant with my first child Kem Ra, both myself and mom had a simultaneous dream where I gave birth to a beautiful dark skinned boy with curly hair. Despite me and Kem Ra's dad being of mid brown complexion, he indeed did come out with beautiful dark skin and very curly hair.

With Omo I had lots and lots of dreams about her. I remember dreaming that one day she was very little and she ran right into our bedroom. In the dream I was shocked because I thought "she is so young to be walking and running". When I woke up from the dream I knew that it seemed to indicate that Omo was going to walk very early. She did. In fact, she was walking and running by 11 months just like my dream.

I would suggest that you keep a dream journal. It could prove an invaluable source of information to draw upon.

Dream Journal Exercise

Keep a Dream Journal. Put a heading and date to your dreams. Spend a little bit of time contemplating what you feel the dream could be indicating to you. The more you record and acknowledge your dreams is the more it seems that your dreams will honor you with more and more information.

The Dance of the Ultra Sound

On a final note. I can't lie. No amount of pampering, scrubbing, massaging, or even having that famous manly massage from hubby or the boyfriend can beat the first ultra sound pictures of the baby or the sound of their heartbeat racing when the doctor rubs that cold gel on your stomach and puts that funny looking hand held thing on it. It all just feels so...worth it! Also I never did believe there was a baby in my stomach until I saw the pics and heard that ever so fast heartbeat. I always doubted my baby girl was there until I heard and saw those things! Maybe, I should have called this book *Forty and In Denial!* Anyway, back to center. Nothing beats pampering more than those ultra sound pictures and noises. They help to reinforce the beautiful dance that life has put us on. Enjoy them.

DANCING THE PATH NOTES

Childbirth provided the drama I craved, the thrill of peeking over the primal edge of creation, the rush of the unexpected.
Peggy Vincent, Baby Catcher

_____

_____

_____

_____

_____

_____

_____

_____

_____

_____

_____

_____

_____

_____

_____

_____

_____

_____

_____

_____

_____

_____

_____

_____

_____

_____

_____

_____

PART THREE

PLOOP!: THE DANCE OF DELIVERY – SAY HELLO TO BABY

Ploop! The Birth

"Nobody told me it would hurt so much!" I screamed through mum's meditation music.

"If they had told me I wouldn't have done this!" I screamed again.

That was fourteen years ago when I was giving birth to Kem Ra.

Now a few weeks before the birth of our baby girl I was getting flashbacks. Terrible flashbacks! Oh, so terrible they would keep me up during the night. Then there were those images that kept on loaming before me of how this birth was going to be. The ones with my feet up in stirrups, surrounded by male doctors grinning endlessly at me, telling me to push against the whole force of gravity loamed before me.

Those re-occurring images made me feel whiny. No, betrayed. No, just sorry for myself. Why couldn't I have that natural birth I wanted? As I got closer to my due date – pain was the only thought on my mind. I was now a pain merchant. I was dishing out pre-pain to myself long before the birth. I didn't want any pain. Maybe, God was really a man, after all. Would a woman give out all this pain? Could God not have thought of a way of leaving the darlings at our front door, a full one year old?

A few weeks before the birth I packed my bags miserably. Miserably, I tell you, because Pain would not leave my head.

"If you concentrate on the pain that is what you will get," wisely stated one author I read.

True, true. I could see what they meant. So I packed my bags for the hospital and tried to gag Pain from my brain. But, it didn't work. The vivid memories and fears kept on creeping back.

"Hi," Pain said to me grinning.

"You cruel beast!" I shouted back.

I continued to pack my bags. Pain was not going to get the best of me. Nope. What was Derrick doing all this time? Trying to be a sane Alpha male. Boy did I put him to the test? How long could Alpha male stay sane? He did pretty well. Here's a sample of one of our testing conversations.

"Baby, I need some meditation music to get me through the pain."

"Okay, I will download some on the MP3 player for you."

"Baby, I think I need one of those massage thingies. They say it helps alleviate the pain."

"No problem. The next time we are at the shopping center we will get one."

"Baby, I better make some pain massage oil. I remember I had some at my birth with Kem. Can you buy me the stuff to make it?"

"I will do that. Just give me the ingredients and website you want to purchase it from."

"Baby, I read in a magazine today that it is good to burn some nice fragrance or have a natural fragrance spray for the birthing room."

"Okay, let's have a look out for one."

"Baby, I was thinking about that meditation music. Do you think the doctors will let me play it in the room?"

"Not sure. I will make sure you can listen to it on the MP3 player."

"Baby, guess what I read in this book today? If I breathe in the right way then I can get through this in one piece. Will you practice with me?"

"Anything to make you happy baby."

"Baby, I need to get a nice nighty for the hospital."

"No probs. Let's get you one."

Maybe, Derrick was half crazy in the face of all my demands and angst. Anyway, it took me a whole seven days to pack that bag. I made a list as well. One I stuck on its inner lid. It was for Derrick, of course, and it read,

"Just in case I go into labor don't forget….."

The thing I was really craving was an acupressure foot board. I read in a book that if you rested and pressed your foot on one you would go into labor immediately. Kem Ra's birth had been only six hours. It was six hours that felt like an eternity though, but it was still a manageable six hours. I know I am scaring you about the pain thing, but when you do all the right things pain is really manageable. I am just scared of pain. Even if a pin pricks me, I am crying with pain.

Two weeks approximately before the due date of August 28th 2011 – I decided to pack some more. I also decided to continue going to the local university library, and to continue my swimming. For six months I had been in the library writing up notes for a book I was working on. Every time I went to the library, I kept on getting these strange nervous looks from the staff (who happened to be good friends of mine and Derrick's.)

Maybe, they were right to be so jittery. Eleven days before my due date I fell asleep in the library. I just didn't realize I was so tired. I woke up to the pitch dark. I got up from the comfy sofa (every pregnant woman's dream) and begun to walk towards the front of the library. I could barely see where I was walking. Goose pimples covered my body. I almost could see a shadow dart across the floor. Then the thought struck me, what if I was locked in? I picked up my pace.

As I approached the front desk I noticed there was a dim light. I moved faster towards the it. It was shining through an office window. There seemed to be a seated figure seated behind a front desk. As I got closer I instantly recognized the form of my archivist friend. Unfortunately, he did not recognize me straight away. I virtually saw him leap several inches of his chair. Eventually, he placed a face to the dark shadow and released a hilarious laugh.

"Lucky. I just happened to be working late tonight," he revealed. "What happened to you?" He enquired.

"Fell asleep on the sofa," I replied embarrassed.

He laughed out aloud again, "wait till I tell the rest about this. You will forever be associated with that sofa. It will be called Omi's sofa!"

I saw the funny side of everything too and laughed with him. Once I got home I shared the whole story with Derrick. He couldn't stop laughing, and laughing, and laughing. It made his day.

Seven days before the labor. I was still swimming. The swimming attendants, just like the library staff, looked very jittery.

I didn't know what everyone was so nervous about. I thought I was going to be way over my due date.

Four days before my due date I began to pester Derrick.

"Do you think they will induce me? I don't want to be induced."

I fess up – I started to cry. Poor Derrick. He tried to console me.

"It's going to be okay, trust me."

I wanted to, but I knew he wasn't God. Also I knew that I had no labor signs.

My fears were not alleviated when went to the doctors that same day.

"Having any symptoms?" he asked.

"Like what?"

"Bloody mucous plug, contractions that make you feel like you're in labor but then they fade of."

"Not really."

Blank stare, an "oh, I see." Followed by a polite smile.

"we won't talk about inducing you just as yet," he eventually said.

I panicked. Induce? There's that word. Induce. No! No! No! Not induce. Instead of voicing my panic I found myself smiling sweetly back at my lovely doctor.

"Ok, doc. We will keep you informed."

"You heard what the doctor said, sweetie. He is talking about inducing," I moaned to Derrick after leaving the doctor's office.

"He wasn't. It will be okay dear."

Derrick was such a trooper. He did all he could to quell my fears.

Three days before the due date. I made the pain balm for my lower back. It made me feel a bit better (even if it was for a small moment). That was until that feeling overtook me again.

"I knew this was going to be a disaster," I cried to Derrick.

"Baby, it will be okay," he tried to ensure again.

What more could the poor man say? I continued to go swimming. It gave me a sense of relief and comfort, even if it didn't do the same for the swimming attendants. They always grinned at me nervously.

"Oh, baby what about if I go into labor and you are at work? Even away?" yet another panicky feeling hit me.

"It will be okay," Derrick reassured never seeming to get tired of my angst.

As the birth date got closer, I decided to take my fear by the neck and empower myself. Instead of panicking I decided it was so much better to find a remedy to the possible extensive pain I was going to feel. The hunt was on for the magic elixir. I hunted high and low through the internet, my herbal books, old college notes. Bingo, I found the   herbal remedies: Red Raspberry, Black Cohosh. Blue Cohosh. All three were remedies that came up over and over again. I decided to check out what my favorite herbalist David Hoffman had to say about them in relation to birthing. I read his website and made copious notes which read something like this:

Raspberry is known to be a gentle and effective astringent, tonic and parturient. It has a long tradition of use in pregnancy as a strengthener and toning agent of the womb tissue helping to assist in contractions and checking any hemorrhaging during labor. It is rich in iron and calcium. You might also be interested in the fact that its astringent qualities makes it very effective in cases of diarrhea, easing mouth problems such as mouth ulcers, bleeding gums, gum inflammations and sore throats.

Blue Cohosh is also a very fascinating herbal remedy. Known as Squawroot. It's botanical name is Caulophylum thalictroides The term Caulophyllum is derived from two Greek words—kaulos, stem; and phullon, leaf. It was given this name because the leaves terminate in such a manner as to give them the appearance of being a mere continuation of the stem. The root and the Rhizome of the plant are used. Renown as an effective uterine tonic, emmenagogue (promotes menstruation), anti-spasmodic, anti-rheumatic and diuretic.

According to leading herbalist David Hoffman Blue Cohosh can be used during all stages of pregnancy. It can be used where there is a weakness or loss of tone in the uterus. It's anti-spasmodic properties makes it an important herbs to use where there is a threatened miscarriage. It will also ease false labor pains. When used just before birth it will aid in an easy delivery.

In the Herbal Priest and Priest it is stated that the following conditions can also be alleviated with the help of Blue Cohosh: rheumatic pain, endometriosis, ovaritis, dysmenorrhoea, urethritis, vaginitis, thrush, restlessness during pregnancy, menopausal pains and discomfort.

Black Cohosh, also known as Black Snakeroot, Bugbane, Rattleroot, Rattleweed and Squawroot is a powerful yet gentle: Emmenagogue, anti-spasmodic, alterative, nervine, hypotensive. It has a potent action as a relaxant and a normalizer of the female reproductive system. It may be used to ease painful or delayed menstruation, Ovarian cramps or cramping pain in the womb. Which makes it helpful for easing the pain of labor. On a wide note It is very good in the treatment of rheumatic pains, but also in rheumatoid arthritis, osteo-arthritis, in muscular and neurological pain. It finds use in sciatica and neuralgia. As a relaxing nervine it may be used in many situations where such an agent is needed.

I was so excited with my finds. I convinced Derrick that I had found the elixir for a pain free labor. A plan began to take shape. I would make a liter of herbal tea, bottle it and bring it to the hospital with me. I would drink it profusely.

"Baby, can we go to Earth Fare, they might have the herbs there?" I suggested to Derrick.

That same day we went to Earth Fare. They didn't have Blue Cohosh or Black Cohosh in stock. However, they had them in tincture form. The cost of the tinctures were beyond our pockets, at that time. Luck of lucks, though. They had Red Raspberry, as a loose herb. I proceeded to buy lots of it.

Initially, when I got home I was happy. Now I was going to have a good labor. Then my worry filled labor flashes came back to haunt me again. Triggering of a deep feeling of angst and negative internal chatter which sounded something like this - *It was really Blue and Black Cohosh that I had wanted. Weren't those my true elixirs?*

On my delivery day. There were no labor signs. No signs at all. At least no signs I recognized. The lack of any signs confirmed my suspicions that I was going to be well overdue. Of course, I complained to poor Derrick,

"What if this baby just keeps on growing and growing in me?"

"Baby, that is not what happens."

"It does if you are overdue!" I shouted irrationally. I couldn't help it but I kept on having flashes of carrying around this big oversized baby in my stomach, and images of my stomach bursting.

The thought was a little disconcerting to say the least. My stomach already felt like I had eaten too much of my favorite Trinidadian dish – roti filled with potato That day I told Derrick that I wanted to go swimming. I thought it would help the baby to arrive.

"Don't think that would be a good idea," he said firmly.

"But, I want to!" I ranted like a big baby.

"You're due today," Derrick reminded me.

"But, I have had no pre-labor signs. I told you it is most probably going to be quite a late baby."

"I want to get the room ready for the baby," he insisted.

"Well, what about Barnes and Nobles?" I asked not wanting to stay at home.

"Okay, let me sort the room out first," Derrick compromised.

Truce reached. I relaxed. Happy with the thought I was going out I began to hum and do an Island cook up of: Red Bean Soup, Curry Turkey, Basmati rice, tropical salad, and carrot juice. You would swear that I was cooking for an army.

I spoke to my mom in London as I prepared the meal. About half an hour into our conversation I began to have some stomach pains. They started getting a little more painful with time. I couldn't handle them and the conversation so I told my mom I would call her back. I thought the pains were pre-labor pains and didn't take them that seriously (even when I got stuck with pain on the back yard step trying to pick some fresh thyme for the soup).

As I went back to the kitchen to cook the cramping pains became more and more intense. Concerned, Derrick told me to time them with his watch as he got my hospital bag and clothes ready. I told him he was panicking and not to worry. I was still convinced I was in pre-labor stages.

When I ended up on my knees Derrick quickly grabbed the watch and said, "How many minutes are they apart?"

"They are about 20 seconds and 1 ½ minutes apart," I replied through gritted teeth.

Okay, I am going to call the doctor," he insisted.

"No, please don't. I don't want to go into hospital early and be induced. Remember the doctor said that we have to wait for the pain to be one minute long and five minutes apart."

"Okay that's it. You need to stop that cooking and I need to call the doctor," Derrick jumped into action.

Luckily I had just finished the cooking.

"No, problem," I said.

As soon as the words had left my mouth I doubled over in pain again and ended up on my knees.

"If only I could give birth like this, on my knees, that would be great," I moaned as another contraction hit me. I checked my contractions they were still not following the doctor's description.

My heart sunk.

"To think I have hours and hours of this to go," I moaned to Derrick.

Another contraction hit me. This time it knocked my breath totally away.

"If only I could chant Om in the hospital room," I teased through the pain. I was feeling well miserable by now.

As I tried to get of my knees another pain hit me. I shouted out, "OMMMMMMMMM!" Instincts told me it would help ease the pain. It did.

"Baby that actually took my pain away!" I informed Derrick excitedly. "It really had helped me."

At that moment I felt as though I had hit on another elixir for a pain free labor. As the pain eased of,

I rose and made myself a cup of Red Raspberry tea and gulped it down. It tasted delicious. Derrick helped me to get down stairs to our bedroom. It was now thirty minutes into the painful waves of contractions. He got me into the bedroom and told me to lie down while he called the doctor. That was the worst advice he could have given. Not his fault. How was he to know that I would have another wave of contractions that would have been pinned me to the bed like a mad axe man.

"I thought I told you to lie down," Derrick reprimanded when he re-entered the room and saw me on my knees.

"I tried, but the contractions felt worse," I moaned.

"The doctor said we need to take you down to the office so that he can see how far you are dilated."

Now the doctor's office was in Rock Hill. A good thirty minutes or more ride away from us. The good news though was that it was a few minutes away from the hospital. So Derrick figured if anything happened it would be okay as we would be near the hospital.

That was all well and good. The only problem was – I couldn't get up of my knees. Every time Derrick tried to get me dressed another wave of contractions would start and pull me down.

"I am sure pre-contractions are not supposed to feel like this!" I screamed.

What happened after that phone call was quick, fast and furious, and it involved quite a bit of heroism. Two minutes after the call to the doctor I felt an unbearable intense pain. It felt as if my waters were about to break. However, after a few seconds I realized it felt more like a baby's head coming down.

"Baby I think the baby is coming! Call the doctor back!!"

"No way sweetie, you just feel like that because the contractions are so intense, just breeeaaaathe!"

I think Derrick could not believe that it was possible for the baby to come so quickly without FAIR notice. There was another bearing down feeling. It was getting kind of scary. I thought something must be going wrong?

After another bearing down feeling I shouted,

"Baby I think you better call 911. This baby is coming right now!"

Derrick took what, he later described in his re-telling of the story, "a quick man-like peak". He raised his head up and reported back.

"I can't see any crowning."

Still he immediately called the doctor back and left a message for a quick call back.

"It's urgent; the baby may be coming now!"

Meanwhile, I took the yelling and screaming to a new level. Eventually Derrick decided to check my repeated claims that the baby was coming more seriously.

He took a second brave look, and he actually noticed something that looked like a head.

By now I was in a daze and in excruciating pain. The pain seemed to just be eating me for dinner.

"Baby just say OMMM!" Derrick said kneeling over me. He knew this had taken my pain away earlier.

"OMMMMMMMMMMMM!" I screamed as the pain whooped me.

Now Om Is meant to be a universal sound that brought creation into being. It has a kind of nice ring about it when you chant it. But there was nothing nice about the ring of my Om. Yes, it was definitely bringing creation into being but not very gracefully.

Derrick massaged my back with what has become his famous Ploop! Massage. Then he proceeded to call 911, threw a few clean white towels under me and began speaking to the emergency dispatcher.

"Baby talk outside if you want to hear them, because I am about to make some noise!" I screamed at Derrick.

"You need a quick response because my wife is having a baby right now!" Derrick shouted down the phone to the Dispatcher.

Within minutes into that conversation an unbearable pain overcame me. Everything went blank. I don't quite remember what happened. I just remember something coming out of me that felt like a full sack of water. I thought it was my waters breaking, but no it was the baby. She plooped out right onto the towels.

"THE BABY IS HERE!," exclaimed Derrick to the dispatcher, me, and the world. He put his phone on speaker, swooped the baby up, dried her off, and began looking for signs of life. I was still kneeling, yes that's right. I gave birth on my knees. I stared at Derrick and the baby in disbelief. No, I didn't bother to say, "I told you so." Derrick handed the baby to me to hold. she was so clean as though someone had washed her. He continued to talk to the dispatcher.

"Is the baby crying?" a calm and commanding voice came out of the phone

"No, she is warm and still," I said.

"Check for her vital signs," the voice commanded gently.

Right then Omololu opened her eyes and looked right at me, then looked around the room, as if to ask, "Where am I?"

Shortly afterwards she took a few gasps of breath. It was all quite an awe inspiring moment.

911 told Derrick to sit tight they would be there as quickly as possible. They gave him further instructions which included to keep the baby warm, and then to find a clean white shoelace. That stumped him. "I mean how many people have a clean shoelace at hand?"

Suddenly he remembered that earlier that day when he had gone into a frenzy of activity cleaning and re-organizing the bedroom he had found a single clean shoe lace and for some reason put it on the bedroom table thinking it would come in handy at some point. It was that very shoe lace he used to tie the baby's umbilical cord. Without that shoelace Derrick always says he doesn't know what damage could have been done to the baby.

Within minutes of Derrick tying the umbilical cord 911 was at the house. They were caring, fast, and efficient. We don't know what we would have done without their swift action. Our neighbor turned up just after them wondering what all the commotion was about. She was sure something had happened to me. You can imagine how shocked she was to see me lying on the floor with an umbilical cord sticking out my nether regions, and a baby in my hands.

The ambulance team got me and the baby into the car. Derrick and Kem Ra followed behind. Everyone headed to the Piedmont hospital in Rock Hill where an equally efficient delivery team from the Woman's Wing acted swiftly to help me deliver her placenta. Although the ambulance team had been worried there might be a complication, the placenta came out no problem.

A few days later our little baby girl was called, Omololu, Iyanu which means "My Child is my Hero / My Blessing" and "Surprise and Miraculous".

We still look back on the labor with wonderment. Kem Ra, most probably with shock and trauma. The whole labor lasted 45 minutes in total. One thing I had forgotten to mention was that the night before the baby came I was belly dancing, because I thought it would help to get the baby out.

Our local South Carolinian paper, The Lancaster News, carried the whole story and kept it more or less close to the Press Release that I and Derrick had written. We wrote a press release about the story because we wanted to say a "big thank you" to all those who helped to make the birth a safe one.

The people we thanked were as follows: Our OB/GYN team, the Lancaster 911 team, the EMS team, Lancaster Fire Department, Glenn A. Raymond, M.D. from the Carolina OB/GYN, the delivery team at Rock Hill's Piedmont Hospital, our neighbor Dr. Stella

Williams who came over immediately to see if everything was okay, and God for the many blessings we received that day.

About eight months latter Pregnancy and New born magazine carried the story in their online magazine *Birth Day* Blog.

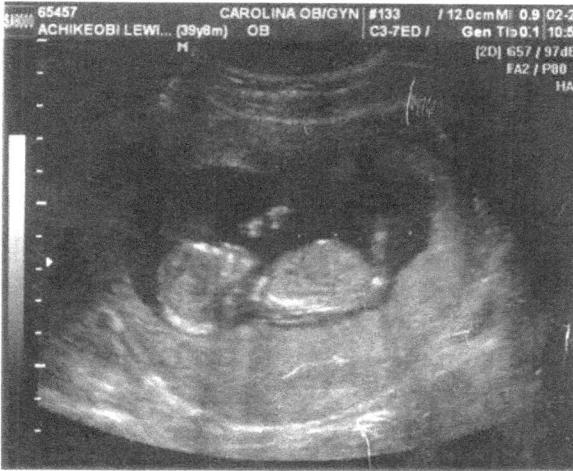

Omo's Ultra Sound

Omo with Omileye and Derrick at just a few hours old

The Dance of a Natural Labor

We may not all enjoy or even want to have a forty five minute delivery. However, the question is perhaps - how can one have something that resembles a beautiful labor dance. One where we are not all strung out, stressed out, and freaked out.

The question may also be - why even think of having a natural labor? Why not just obliterate the pain with an epidural? Why not just let the doctors just do it all for us?

According to all the research I have encountered and personal experience a natural labor gives us a feeling of more grace, control, joy and happiness about our birthing process. If you want a natural birthing, The American Pregnancy Association reveal that these days there are more women, like us, who are aiming for birth the natural way.

If you are thinking you would like to have a birth at home they reveal that a home birth costs about 60% less than a hospital birth. It also provides:

- Immediate bonding and breastfeeding. Early breastfeeding helps mom stop bleeding, clear mucus from the baby's nose and mouth, and transfer disease-fighting antibodies in the milk from mother to baby.

- Allows you to be surrounded with those you love. When you include children, family, and friends in the birth process, it provides you with many helpers and allows a very intimate bonding experience for everyone involved.

- Comfort for those who want to avoid episiotomy, cesarean section, epidural and other interventions.

Apparently it is a good idea to get a doula if you are looking to have a homebirth. If you are wondering what on earth one of those looks like. Well, the Doula Association of Southern California (DASC) has quite a nice little description of one:

Doula is an ancient Greek word most commonly translated as female maidservant. A doula in today's world is a trained and experienced woman who accompanies a new mother through birth and/or the postpartum period, offering emotional support, physical comfort, practical assistance and non-medical care.

In other words they are those brave souls who replace the traditional role of grandma sitting in the corner and meditating with you. Or maybe they are also the brave souls who sit right alongside grandmother and strengthen whatever process helps you have a great birthing.

Even if you are going to opt for a hospital birth I believe, along with the rest of the natural birthing fraternity, you can still dance your way joyfully through a natural birthing experience. No, really, you can. Just follow some of the tips in the following pages, do lots of research about birthing tips and get your partner on board. The more you empower yourself is the more you can have a birthing experience you can love.

Now I just want to mention something about epidurals. I know you may also think you really need one. I know we all hate pain. I know you may also be thinking that your body, mind and soul can get through the whole process without something to numb the pain. Yet, they can. Look how I got through my forty five minute birth. My body literally took charge, and successfully so. With some preparation, and good support you can dance right through that birth.

You may be interested to note that experts agree that epidurals and other pain relieving medications often lead to a slower delivery. Pain medications often interfere with the body's natural way of laboring and can slow down contractions. This increases total laboring periods. In addition, women often do not feel their contractions and do not know when to push. By not pushing at key times, or with adequate strength, they are not able to facilitate the laboring process. They miss important opportunities to work with the rhythms of their bodies.

Because epidurals disconnect women from the natural pushing action and prolong labor, doctors are prone to intervene in the slowed birthing process and may give a pitocin drip (a uterine stimulant) or use a vacuum or forceps to move the fetus through the birth canal. In addition, fetal monitoring may be necessary to study the fetus's heart rate. This usually requires an instrument to be attached to the baby's scalp. If there are issues related to the heart beat or other complications, a Cesarean-section may be done.

Although epidural use doesn't always cause these complications, it does increase the likelihood that interventions will be used.

Also I know the doctors may have given you the impression that you have to get those legs up into the good old stirrups. Guess what? That simply is not true. There are other options which are highly recommended. As I mentioned at the beginning of this book a great article in the May 2010 issue of Parenting Magazine reveals experts agree that if you are "aiming for a natural birth experience. You don't have to take it lying down."

Then they quote Mayer Eisenstein, M.D., an obstetrician in Chicago who states that upright positions may help you labor faster and deliver your baby sooner because you're not working against gravity. Also we are told,

"Being upright helps move your baby down into your pelvis, and the pressure of his head against your cervix encourages dilation. Standing also helps expand your pelvic inlet, the bony opening through which your baby's head first passes. If you choose to have an epidural, you'll probably have to lie down at that point, but some of these positions may also be useful before then."

They further state that the best positions to adopt are: sitting, squatting, on your hands and knees or any posture your body wants to take.

Dancing With the Birth Plan

I didn't have one. Well, I didn't have one written down. I think I got put off by one of the nurses when I went for my doctor's visit. I mentioned the birth plan (blame those baby magazines). She looked at me and said "with all honesty, don't do it. Doctors get really funny about it." She was just being honest and I appreciated it. The only thing is that I followed her advice and didn't write one.

However, when I think about it, I had one all up in my head. If I had written my Birth Plan down it would have read something like this:

- *I don't want any doctors present*
- *I don't want any nurse around me who is not going to be fully supportive and positive of my wishes*
- *I want the whole thing to feel like a home birth*
- *I want Om Mani Padme Hum playing and floating through the roam*
- *I want to chant as a form of pain killer*
- *The atmosphere must be really conducive with candle lights*
- *I want to be lovingly supported as I give birth on my knees*
- *I don't want anyone trying to take me out of the kitchen cupboard if I try to give birth there*
- *I definitely don't want no epidural (only if the pain gets too agonizing)*
- *I want God to make it really quick!*

Now this is where the warning comes in. Be careful what you ask for. You will notice from my birth story I got most of what I asked for. So how unplanned was my birth! It seems that someone up there was listening. Pregnancy Today revealed why a birth plan is a good idea,

"A lot of moms have decided that they would like to have a say in the matter, and have created birth plans to serve that purpose. Such a plan is a simple and non-confrontational way for you to make your preferences for your pregnancy and birth clear to everyone who will be with you on the big day (or days, as the case may be). There are so many choices to make and things to consider - from whether or not you want to have anesthesia to how long you want to stay after the birth - that making your voice heard is important. Every hospital and every health care professional does something just a little bit differently, and without a plan, you may be given the "default" settings - whatever they might be."

They further remind us that,

"A birth plan is a statement of preferences, not a binding contract. If you change your mind about something - such as the need for anesthesia, who else is allowed in the labor suite, rooming-in or breastfeeding - those wishes should be respected."

"Even the best birth plan won't take the place of self-education or good communication with your doctor or midwife, but it

*may help you move a few steps forward on the way to a
rewarding birth experience and fond memories of your child's
entry into the world."*

The Dance of the Labor Breath

Breath is the gift of life. So the saying goes. Nowhere
does this show up more true than during the labor
dance. Breath has the power of helping us to work and
align ourselves with our body intuition.

The American Pregnancy Association has some
great information on breathing that is worth taking a
note of. The association helps us to understand the
meaning of what patterned breathing during labor
means. According to the association it "simply means
breathing at any number of possible rates and depths."
They explain that some women prefer breathing deeply,
using their diaphragm to fill their abdomen with air.
While others prefer light breathing, inhaling just enough
to fill their chest. They encourage each woman to find
breathing patterns that calm and relax her. According to
the association "breathing should be at a comfortable
rate and not cause you to feel short of breath or light-
headed." The more a woman learns about labor and
birth, the more she will see how different patterns of
breathing are used at different stages.

Benefits of Patterned Breathing

They further explain that patterned breathing is helpful
when experiencing various types of pain, discomfort,

anxiety or fear. It has many benefits which include the following:

- Breathing becomes an automatic response to pain
- Mom remains in a more relaxed state and will respond more positively to pain
- The steady rhythm of breathing is calming during labor
- Provides a sense of well-being and a measure of control
- Provides more oxygen, which provides more strength and energy for mother and baby
- Brings purpose to each contraction, making them more productive
- Patterned breathing and relaxation become habits for life's every day stressors

Getting Started With Patterned Breathing

They make the following good point about how to begin practicing patterned breathing, stating that traffic jams, headaches, and household chores provide opportunities to practice different breathing techniques and make them part of your routine. One great tip they share is "to simulate labor, some child birth educators suggest holding an ice cube in your hand to practice effective breathing techniques during momentary pain."

How to Breath at Different Stages of Labor

First Stage

They recommend the following breathing patterns for the first stage of labor:

- Slow breathing for intense contractions
- Light accelerated breathing during the active phase of labor: This is where you breath in and out rapidly through your mouth at one breath per second. The breath is kept shallow and light. Inhalations are kept quiet and exhalations are clearly audible); variable (transition) breathing. Which is a variation of light breathing. It is sometimes referred to as "pant-pant-blow" or "hee-hee-who" breathing.
- Variable breathing combines light shallow breathing with a periodic longer or more pronounced exhalation. Variable breathing is used in the first stage if you feel overwhelmed, unable to relax, in despair, or exhausted.
- For breathing to avoid pushing at the wrong time they advise: Avoid holding your breath, but to breathe in and out constantly or raising your chin and blowing or panting. This will keep you from adding to the pushing that your body is already doing.

Second Stage of Labor

During the second stage of labor they recommend what is called Expulsion Breathing. This is done once the cervix is fully dilated and the second stage of labor has begun. The directions for Expulsion Breathing are as follows:

1) Take an organizing breath — a big sigh as soon as the contraction begins. Release all tension (go limp all over — head to toe) as you breathe out.

2) Focus on the baby moving down and out, or on another positive image.

3) Breathe slowly, letting the contraction guide you in accelerating or lightening your breathing as necessary for comfort. When you cannot resist the urge to push (when it "demands" that you join in), take a big breath, tuck chin to chest, curl your body and lean forward. Then bear down, while holding your breath or slowly releasing air by grunting, moaning or other verbalizing. Most important of all, relax the pelvic floor. Help the baby come down by releasing any tension in the perineum.

4) After 5-6 seconds, release your breath and breathe in and out. When the urge to push takes over join in by bearing down. How hard you push is dictated by your sensation. You will continue in this way until the contraction subsides. The urge to push comes and goes in waves during the contraction. Use these breaks to breathe deeply providing oxygen to your blood & sufficient oxygen for the baby.

5) When the contraction ends, relax your body and take one or two calming breaths.

Avoiding Dry Mouth

They also give some good tips how to alleviate dry mouth during labor:

- Touch the tip of your tongue to the roof of your mouth just behind your teeth as you breathe. This slightly moistens the air you breathe.
- With your fingers spread, loosely cover your nose and mouth so that your palm reflects the moisture from your breath.
- Sip fluids or suck on ice chips between contractions
- Brush your teeth or rinse your mouth with mouth wash periodically.

The association recommend that you use and switch between Patterned Breathing techniques according to your own body wisdom. During my first pregnancy knowing the Patterned Breathing helped me to get through six and half hours of labor time and pain. However, as you know my second pregnancy was so fast, I did not have time to even think about breathing. Everything went so 45 minutes fast that I had no choice but to let that inner wisdom guide me and thank God it did!

The Dance of the Mantra!

I remember my new friend Beth Robertson, a beautiful Navajo sister who is an experienced doula, Master Weaver who helps people weave the healing into their lives stated to me she has observed that "each woman has her own birthing mantra".

I think she is right. When I gave birth to Omo I naturally chanted Om. It is interesting to note that is the mantra that Omo still loves to chant even now at twenty months.

Beth believes the labor mantra or sound we often chant or make during the birthing process is often the same one our baby will tend to repeat and gravitate towards. Once again, I think she is right.

Making sounds during labor seems to be the natural sound that emanates from a deep primordial place within us. It is the sound that our inner midwife most probably feels will really help us through the birthing and labor stages we have to go through..

So feel free. Go ahead and make them. For myself I have found that Om is a good mantra in all stages of our dance with life. It is very healing and I have found that it helps to clear pain.

Breathing Reminders

First & Active Stage of Labor
Intense Pain: Slow Breathing
Active Stage of labor: Light Accelerated Breathing
Overwhelmed: Variable Breathing
General: Basic Meditation Breathing (use when as and when your inner wisdom dictates)
General Pain alleviation: Sound Meditation

Second Stage of Labor
Dilated Cervix: Expulsion Breathing

Follow Your Inner Wisdom
Switch between breathing patterns as the pain and your body dictates and don't worry it will! As you can see from my story birth has this strange way of taking on its own life. So yes, follow that intuition.

The Dance of Comfort Massage and Labor Comfort Strategies

As my labor sped through a record 45 minutes I found that my husband massaging and applying considerable pressure to my lower back with his "Ploop Massage" technique was one of the best things that really helped to alleviate my pain. We are also convinced that it helped the baby to ploop right on out!

So what do we need to know about massage during the labor stage? Well according to an article in Midwifery Today called *The Primal Touch of Birth: Midwives, Mothers and Massage* by Kara Maia Spencer, LMT traditional midwives and wise women were often the "barefoot doctors" of their tribe or village. The traditional midwife was a holistic practitioner integrating knowledge of herbs, massage techniques, spiritual healing and maternal health care.

She found that the midwives of Jamaica have elaborate massage routines for every stage of labor. The Jamaican midwife may rub the woman's abdomen with toona leaves, massage the body with olive oil and ease transition pains by patting the belly with a warm, damp rag.

While Zapotec midwives of southwest Mexico accurately detect the position of the fetus against the spine through massaging the pregnant mother's legs and evaluating tension and vital energy flow. Mayan uterine massage, practiced by granny healers and midwives, encourages reproductive health and enhances childbearing. The Yucatan midwife gives a routine *sobada* (massage) during each visit with the mother. The majority of business to be had at a prenatal or postpartum visit occurs during the *sobada*: discussion, counseling, recommendations and diagnosis.

Then the Seventeenth-century English midwives used oil of lilies to massage laboring women. Malaysian mothers massage their navels with coconut oil to encourage the baby to descend. Japanese midwives practice acupressure, shiatsu and foot and leg massage during labor. *Samba,* the traditional Japanese word for "midwife," translates as "the elderly women who massages." Modern midwives and doulas use sacral counterpressure and pelvic presses to ease low back pain and open the pelvis during labor.

She further states that in cultures all over the world, midwives and mothers have massaged and oiled the perineum to increase elasticity and used fundal massage to help the uterus contract during labor and after the birth of the placenta.

Now I know that all that Kara Maia Spencer, LMT shares is true, for I remember my mother who hails from Jamaica telling me various massages to do for my stomach and perineum. I also know that even for when the baby has just been birthed Jamaican and Caribbean elders put the baby through an elaborate set of massages for strengthening and creating flexibility in their bodies and limbs.

So from all that has been shared we can see that massage during the pregnancy and labor process has a highly held place. During labor, tense muscles can cause excessively painful contractions. Massage techniques help to relax muscles decreasing the sensation of pain. It also helps to combat the Fear-Tension-Pain Cycle. Firm pressure is very good for helping to alleviate pain, especially to the lower back. But generally, anywhere there is pain apply pressure in the form of pressure strokes and presses.

Whoever is going to massage you inform them that according to www.birthnaturally.net, the "laboring woman does not want you to start touching her after the contraction has begun. Nor does she want you to rub her back for a few seconds, then rub her arm, then move back to her neck. Both of these mistakes will cause her to become distracted and she will feel more pain than is necessary." They recommend that the person chooses a touch pattern and a part of the body that needs focusing on and continue that touch through several contractions. So tell them to exercise beforehand!

They also give further good advice by stating it is important for the individual who is giving you the massage to allow you to find a position that is comfortable for you. Then they should contort themselves to reach which ever area of your body is feeling the most tension.

While giving birth to Omololu I found being on my knees helped me with my labor pains as they came on thick and fast!

Also a hand massager to your lower back and tension spots is a great way to alleviate pain. Along with my massage oil the *Labor Ease Massage Oil* given in the section on: *Herbs and Aromatherapy for Labor*.

What about those additional comfort strategies? I found that the pregnancy magazines were filled with great suggestions. But, here is a great list of comfort strategies that I came across on ivillage.com:

Comfort Strategies

Environment:
dim lights
peaceful surroundings
warmth
Music

Physical:
walking
pelvic rocking
positioning pillows for comfort
slow dancing with partner
sitting on birth ball and swaying
lifting up the abdomen

Touch:
massage
stroking
cuddling
counter pressure against lower back
Acupressure

Heat:
deep tub bath
shower
ice packs on lower back
cool cloth to wipe face

Cognitive:
visualization
focusing on the breath
structured breathing patterns
Aromatherapy

Labor companion:
Doula & or Partner

Labor Ease Massage Oil

Ingredients
1 cup of oil (sunflower, soya, olive or almond)
10 drops of Geranium Oil
10 drops of Rosemary Oil
10 drops of chamomile

Directions
Pour into bottle, shake and massage into areas where you most need to alleviate the pain and tension

The Ploop Massage

Directions

Locate your partners lower back and begin to exert firm pressure on either side of the spine with your thumbs and fingers.
We found that this really helped to ease some of the bearing down pressure away, and we now believe it helped to deliver the baby in record time.

Massage Reminders

Have someone present to massage you

Applying pressure on the lower back helps to "Ploop" the pain away

Do not be forced into an uncomfortable position while in labor. Let the person contort their body to how you are positioned. So tell them to get exercising before the big day!

Strokes, kneading, pressing done with pressure all help alleviate the pain

Don't forget your Labor Ease Massage Oil!

Dancing the Blessingway

I want to make a special mention of the Blessingway ritual, because I wish I had one, but I didn't. I found out about Blessingway ceremonies for birthing, after the fact. A Blessingway is a beautiful and special wonderful ritual for the mother-to-be. It helps her to celebrate her steps into motherhood.

Many believe that the Blessingway tradition was begun by Native Americans. What I love about the Blessingway is that it was traditionally a ritual to offer blessing at many life passages, not just pregnancy. Because so many moms struggle with post pregnancy I would suggest a Blessingway for moms who have delivered.

For a Blessingway ceremony, friends and relatives of the mother come together to give her support and encouragement as she waits for labor to begin. This type of support can really get us birthing moms through the challenging stages of the whole labor process. Here are some ideas for how to hold a Blessingway ritual. I got this from a lovely website www.naturalbirthandbabycare.com:

Prayers, Poems, and Blessings: a traditional way to bless somebody is to say a prayer for them, to write and/or read a poem for them, or to say or find a special blessing for them. Something of this nature is ideal for a Blessingway. You can ask each participant to bring something they've found or written to bless the mother.

You can compile the prayers/poems/blessings into a small, beautiful journal or notebook for the mother. If some prayers are going to be created on the spot you could record with a small tape recorder and later transcribe them to be given to the mother.

Beads: This is my favorite Blessingway tradition. It is so simple and anybody can do this, even if they cannot attend the Blessingway. Have each person invited bring or send a bead that they have picked for the mother. The bead should be something the guest has picked with the mother in mind.

At the blessingway string all the beads onto a cord for the mother to wear during labor. Many mothers have said that these birth beads give them strength and focus during labor. It is a powerful and tangible way to show your love and the community support that surrounds the mother.

Belly Cast: A belly cast is a fun activity that can be done at the blessingway. Many mothers enjoy having a belly cast done. It's a slightly messy and light-hearted activity that will bring smiles to everyone. It also gives the mother a lovely keepsake of her body full of baby. Later the mom can decorate the belly cast however she likes, or she can leave it simple and untouched.

Belly Painting: Another fun activity is to paint the mother's belly. You can use henna paints or any non-toxic (preferably natural) body paints. The mother may have a design she would like, something of special significance. You can talk it over with the mother beforehand and decide what she would like. Henna paint may work especially well because it could last until the birth, if the mother wants.

Lighting Candles: Lighting a candle at the blessingway is a lovely way to bring a sacred feel to the atmosphere. Or you can ask each guest to bring a candle to light during their blessing for the mother. Afterwards each guest will take her candle home and light it when she hears the mother is in labor.

Washing Feet and Brushing Hair: Washing a mother's feet in warm water gently scented by essential oils is a lovely way to show support for her. Many mothers also love to have their hair brushed. This feminine activity is very soothing and empowering to the mother.

Make "Help" Lists: Though not truly part of the ceremony, you should consider having each guest write down a meal that they are committed to bringing for the mother after her baby is born. Alternately each guest can bring a pre-made frozen meal, if the mother has space in her freezer. Each guest should also sign up for a period of housework in the days after the baby is born.

You or another guest take responsibility for organizing and overseeing the help. The mother shouldn't have to do anything. At the blessingway tell her of your plans and assure her you have it all taken care of.

You will be amazed how much this simple gift of food and time will bless the mother and her child. It is a gift given with a servant's heart, and it brings peace, love, and joy to the new family.

DANCING THE PATH NOTES

If we are to heal the planet, we must begin by healing birthing.
Agnes Sallet Von Tannenberg

PART FOUR

THE DANCE OF POST PREGNANCY

Baby Say Hello to the World

The Dance Continues

When I had Kem Ra, my first child, my mom immediately moved in the house and planted herself there for almost two months. She shared in the cooking cleaning, and made sure I was alright. Being in my mid twenties, and in a relationship I was like, "mom do you think it is time to leave?" Ahh, the follies of youth. After two months she did leave and all hell broke loose. With no help from my son's father, and my mom living a couple of hours drive away from me I was left to cope on my own. Worn to a frazzle I became a weepy mass of crying regrets.

When I had Omo, my second child, Derrick her father was there all the way (he still is). However, I didn't have the beautiful supportive presence of my mother. She was all the way in London and me – all the way in South Carolina, US. The day I came home from the hospital I cooked for the whole family, and my family duties proceeded and continued full steam ahead. Within two months of coming home with Omo, and in between the demands of: family responsibilities, looking after a new baby, adjusting to motherhood the second time round, trying to continue my creative/career pursuits, and breast feeding – I came down with six eye ulcers which happened one after the other. The worst thing about it all - I had to continue doing all of the above. To say I was an overwhelmed frazzle, would not be no exaggeration.

To make matters even worse, other new moms seemed to be coping so gracefully that it made me feel quite inadequate. It was not until I began to speak to other moms, and begin to see clients (many of whom were new moms) again for my healing wellness practice that I realized that many moms were just as exhausted and overwhelmed as me. I also came to realize that many new moms suffered their lot in silence.

In all this stark reality I looked back on my first birth experience and realized how much I missed my mom's presence. I came to appreciate the Caribbean tradition which my mom was living by. The tradition that supports the new mother for months and months after she has given birth. This support is often provided by the woman's mother or a female elder in her or her husband's family.

Which brings me to the next point, when the women are supported the men also get a break. For there are many men today, like Derrick, who are 100 percent involved in the looking after of the baby. These wonderful loving fathers, and partners get totally worn out, as well. Imagine two worn people and a baby – that's not a good combo.

I truly want all new moms, and dad's to feel "Lifted Up to the Sky" as Lori Portka's front cover picture implies in such a beautiful way. So here is some of the wisdom I have learned and shared along the way. Much of it I base on the Seven Principles of Wellness, along with all my experience of being a new mom. In fact, I would suggest that you look back over the section: The Dance of Fertility for more details on the Seven Principles of Wellness. For the beautiful thing is that the principles (as detailed in that section) can be used for any stage of birthing to good effect.

Lift Her Up to the Sky List (Men, you too share in this advice):

- **Be kind:** Be kind to yourself. Know that at the beginning you will not be able to do all that you had done previously, but your life isn't over. Trust me, it isn't. Little by little you can begin to shape your new reality like a potter molding the clay. The time of being a new mom offers us the opportunity to truly reflect on the things that are valuable in our lives, our talents, our gifts, and the things we really want out of life.

- **Embrace the Struggle in the Dance:** Even though this stage is a dance too (like all the others), there will be a bit of struggle involved. This is natural as we are birthing into a new powerful reality. My beautiful Navajo sister friend Beth told me that in their culture they have a holy one called Changing Woman. She represents the different stages and phases of our lives. If we see this stage as another part of the process of being Changing Women, then we can embrace this moment as one that offers the opportunity for beautiful growth.

- **Take Time Out:** You must carve time out for yourself. You must, you must. Try and do that on a daily basis. Never give up your creativity or inner self. Nourish that which you are and that which you are becoming. Even taking ten minutes to have a soak in the bath is a good thing for nourishment of the soul. Also I have found that doing some form of creative activity, small or little, is a good way to hold onto one's sanity, peace, and soul.

- **Meditate:** Now this is interesting advice, because I have found that it is hard to continue my meditation practice with new born Omo. But guess what Motherhood opens up a whole new ability to be very creative. Meditation allows us to gather ourselves back together. Just five minutes can make a difference to our souls. I have found the best time and place for me to meditate is when I am lying in bed breast feeding Omo. I often fall asleep, but I wake up feeling so much better. Plus I have crazy wonderful dreams that help me to keep on believing in life!

- **Stretch:** Find time to stretch even a few minutes. Stretching will help you move stagnant energy and nourish and detangle the nervous system. It helps to re-energize the whole mind-body system. What I love with the Bhumi Drum Energy Dance is that mom's can do it even with the baby on their back and crawling between their feet (now we know babies often do those things, don't we?!)

- **Eat Well:** It is really hard for us moms to get those nourishing meals in, so here's some cheat advise – Juice, juice, juice. In the Islands we make a lot of juices. We stretch it all out with some milk (soy milk is what I use), and honey. You can juice and create a liter of it by adding some milk and honey. I would suggest this because us moms with young babies just do not have the time to juice every day. Add green food to the juice (this will give you a wonderful strengthening boost). Juicing will also help us keep the weight of, as it keeps us away from snacking on junk. Which brings me to another point try and have lots of healthy snacks around: fruit, yoghurts, steamed vegetables, hummus, gluten free crackers etc etc

- **Self Massage:** Self massage can be a life saver for us moms. It is a way to stay in shape, keep the energy flowing, and bringing on the peace/calm. (Look in the section: Dance of Fertility for Self Massage advice).

- **Make Time for Intimacy:** It is hard to do this, but making time for intimacy is very important. Sometimes intimacy can just be to cuddle up together. The beautiful thing is that if we allow ourselves (both women and men) to embrace this dance of birthing our dialogue of what intimacy really is opens up. Rather than being a relationship downer, our relationships can find a new self definition. For this to happen both partners have to be kind, loving, open and caring about themselves and the other. Men just a note: If you massage your partners and help with the family chores, guess what? You may have a wife in some sexy lingerie that night faster than you can blink an eye.

The Dance of Remedies

So here is where I share with you some more remedies and things I did along the way that allowed me to dance to the glory of my inner mother. To help you to dance too, I want to first share some beautiful poetic words that that Beth, my Navajo sister friend, shared with me just recently. It was all about Changing Woman and I think they are words that are apt for this part of the journey (every part really):

Changing Woman moves around the circle of life like to quarters of the day, seasons of the year and the milestones of our lives. She is White Shell Woman the white dawn of day, spring and the growth from infancy to puberty. She is Turquoise Woman the full empowerment of the noonday sun, summer time in full bloom into womanhood. She is Abalone Shell Woman the maturity of twilight the autumn of womanhood. She is Black Jet Woman, nighttime, winter of her life and she weathers the cold with an inner warmth for all who come near her.

Dance of the Placenta

In Caribbean culture we have a tradition of burying the placenta of a child under a tree. That placenta is said to nourish new life, and therefore bring luck and wealth to the baby.

Even though in Western medicine the placenta is just seen as a waste product of birthing, other cultures treat the placenta as something that is sacred, spiritually and physically nourishing.

Among the Navajo Indians of the Southwest, it's customary to bury a child's placenta within the sacred Four Corners of the tribe's reservation as a binder to ancestral land and people. New Zealand's Maoris have the same tradition of burying the placenta within native soil. In their native language, the word for land and placenta are the same: whenua. The Ibo of Nigeria and Ghana treat the placenta as the dead twin of the live child and give it full burial rites.

In some cultures the placenta is eaten. Eating the placenta is known as placentophagy. Most mammals in the animal world, including many primates, eat their placentas. This excludes the majority of humans.

Preparing the placenta for consumption by mothers is considered traditional among Vietnamese and Chinese people. The Chinese believe a nursing mother should boil the placenta, make a broth, and then drink it to improve her milk.

A new placenta eating trend is arising amongst Western mothers. Some say that it has helped them to avoid post natal depression. A whole discussion to do with placenta eating was triggered of recently when actress January Jones admitted to People magazine that she had eaten hers, as part of a healthy post natal routine. In a report for ABC new Dr. David Katz, founder of the Yale Prevention Center shared this about placenta eating,

"There is certainly a potential medicinal use. This is a time-honored cultural practice of eating the placenta. It is nutrient-rich and a source of hormones."

As more and more moms and dads opt for natural birth methods, and having ceremonies which gives this special moment in their lives a special significance - the question of what to do with the placenta arises more and more. As myself and Derrick were in the process of moving when Omo was born, we put her placenta in the freezer. It is still there waiting for us to decide on what to do with it.

You too may be left wondering about cord cutting and placenta ceremonies you could do. If you feel drawn to performing a traditional ceremony you have seen or read about, then go right ahead and do so. However, ensure that you give it special touches that make it relevant to you, partner and those involved. Here are some cord cutting and placenta ceremony suggestions:

- Cutting your own cord: To signify the ending of your pregnancy and the beginning of her mothering

- Let your partner cut the cord: to signify participation in the birth, or evidence of their support, or acknowledgement of becoming a family?

- Let the older sibling cut the cord: To signify their acknowledging and accepting the baby into the family or signifying their participation in this important family event

- Bury the placenta by a tree: This could symbolize the beginning of new life, the continual health, and wealth of the child. It could also symbolize the child's connection to the land. If you want to you could bury the placenta in a pot containing a plant or sapling tree. This is can be a good, because the pot can move with you. If you are burying the placenta it should be buried at least 40 cm or more deep.

- Eating your placenta: Apparently there is no real risk of eating your own placenta, but there is a risk of eating someone else's. There are plenty of recipes on line, as to how to prepare a placenta for eating. Some of the more popular ones are seasoning the placenta like and cooking it into a lasagna or stew. There is also the process of dehydrating the placenta and encapsulating it. If I was ever going to eat the placenta I think the latter is the process I would prefer.

Here's some placenta recipes I found on www.about.com. There are plenty abound on the internet.

Roast Placenta

- 1-3lb fresh placenta (must be no more than 3 days old)
  1 onion
  1 green or red pepper (green will add colour)
  1 cup tomato sauce
  1 sleeve saltine crackers
  1 tspn bay leaves
  1 tspn black pepper
  1 tspn white pepper
  1 clove garlic (roasted and minced)

Method

- (Preheat oven to 350 degrees)
- Chop the onion and the pepper & crush the saltines into crumbs.
  2. Combine the placenta, onion, pepper, saltines, bay leaves, white and black pepper, garlic and tomato sauce.
  3. Place in a loaf pan, cover then bake for one and a half hours, occasionally pouring off excess liquid.
  4. Serve and enjoy!

Placenta Cocktail

Ingredients:

1/4 cup fresh, raw placenta
8oz V-8 juice
2 ice cubes
1/2 cup carrot

Method: blend at high speed for 10 seconds. Serve. A tasty thirst quencher!

Placenta Dehydration

- Cut off the cord and membranes.
- Steam the placenta, adding lemon grass, pepper and ginger to the steaming water. The placenta is "done" when no blood comes out when you pierce it with a fork.
- Cut the placenta into thin slices (like making jerky) and bake in a low-heat oven (200-250 degrees F), until it is dry and crumbly (several hours).
- Crush the placenta into a powder - using a food processor, blender, mortar and pestle, or by putting it in a bag and grinding it with rocks.
- Put the powder into empty gel caps (available at drug and health food stores) or just add a spoonful to your cereal, blender drink, etc.

Dance of the Yoni

The last time I had a baby was fifteen years ago. So when I had Omo I was quickly reminded how much it hurt down there. I was slightly torn and beyond sore. Every time I got up to walk I resembled a penguin, and felt like an out and out war hero. Well, as pain is not my forte, I quickly rang my herbalist Allen in London. He suggested the following herbal bath that healed me within one day.

The Herbal Bath that Saved my Yoni (Nether Region)

Ingredients
1 cup of Nettle
1 cup of Calendula
1 cup of Epsom salt

Directions
Simmer dry herbs in a medium pot of water for fifteen minutes. Strain. Add to bath with Epsom Salt. Soak in bath for up to half an hour everyday until you feel less sore. After one soak I had no more pain where I was stitched. I kept on using this bath for a few weeks about three times for the week. It made me feel refreshed and reinvigorated.

Dance of the Poop

After giving birth to Omo I couldn't poop for almost a week. I think part of it was the fear of suffering more pain down there. After a week of feeling completely stopped up inside, I decided to follow my intuition. I made a Soothing Butt Balm and Derrick gave me his famous Ploop! massage. This time it was the poop he was trying to Ploop! Did it all work? Let's just say I am here to tell the tale!

The Essential Butt Balm

The name may sound nasty to the average person but not to us moms with sore bums. Trust me the first pooh hurts. This balm helped to ease all that pain in my bum and helped the poop to ploop right on out! Along with Derrick's Ploop! Massage. Remember for the Ploop! massage you just massage the very end of the lower back with firm pressure.

Ingredients

1 cup of oil (Soy, Olive, Almond or Sunflower)
1 teaspoon of Vitamin E
10 drops of chamomile essential oil
Just a few drops of glycerin
Two table spoons of bees wax

Directions

Place all ingredients in bowl over simmering water. When the beeswax melts pour mixture into smaller bowl. Allow to cool at room temperature. Stir the mixture until a softened balm. Add 10 drops of chamomile. If mixture is not hard enough re-melt and add more bees wax and allow to cool again. Using it is easy. Just massage gently around anus and voila it will go a long way to a pain free toilet experience. It will also help aid in the healing of your stitches.

The Dance of Energy

I mentioned earlier how low my energy was after plooping Omo out, and how I got some of my energy back. Here's the life saver herbal tea that I made to get my energy back. It worked straight away.

Very Revitalizing Tea

Ingredients
4 tablespoons of Nettles
2 tablespoons of Lemongrass

Directions
Simmer all ingredients in small pot of water for fifteen minutes. Strain. Add milk and honey to taste. Nettle herb is renowned for its restorative, tonic properties and profuse amounts of iron. Lemongrass adds a tasty and balancing tone to this combo. This tea helped me feel so much more uplifted and stronger. Remember you can store any excess in the fridge.

The Dance of the Earth Mother Body

Even though we shouldn't, and even though it seems taboo the truth is many of us worry about our weight after pregnancy. Us women always want to look and feel good about ourselves, and so we should. We need to be kind to ourselves and know that the weight will drop of slowly but surely. There are also things we can do that will ensure it does not get unnecessarily added to. Here are a few I can share with you:

- **Kindness:** I always mention this, because it is something we should never forget – be kind to yourself.

- **Juicing:** (look at beginning of this section and at the Dance of Fertility for more details about some easy juicing).

- **No Eating Big meals after 6pm** – the body has a clock. The best time to eat our largest meal is between 12 to 4 pm. That is when the body is at its metabolic height. After 6 pm the body does not do much digesting. The key is to eat light after this time. Think soups, steamed vegetables, small amounts of food etc.

- **Eat balanced meals:** wherever possible eat a plate that looks something like: 50% Carbohydrates, 40% Protein, 10% health fats. Eating balanced meals helps us to stop snacking on junkie foods.

- **Cook in bulk:** For quite sometime after birthing us new moms just don't have time to cook, so aim to cook in bulk. Cook meals that can last a couple of days.

- **Self Massage:** will help to keep body toned, fat down, and energy up.

- **Meditation:** Fit a few minutes in each day to keep centered.

- **The Goddess Bath:** 1 cup of sea salt, 1 cup of Epsom salt will help you break a sweat and lighten up the toxins, emotional and physical fatigue.

- **Bhumi Drum Energy Dance:** Doing even one round of the Jala Chandra Namaskar (Water Moon Salutation) routine of the Bhumi Drum Energy Dance (put in lots of hip rotations) can definitely help to keep our Earth Mother bodies toned. Find the routine in the Dance of Pregnancy section.

The Dance of Breast Feeding

I couldn't help it. Memories floated in front of me. Ones of cracked sore nipples for the first three weeks of my last pregnancy. Ouch. They hurt. Deep down I did want to breastfeed Omo, but those memories wouldn't go away. Now forty, I wasn't sure if I would have the patience and the resilience to bear the pain for sooooooo long, again. Surely the bottle would be so much easier.

Eventually, the decision was made. I would breastfeed her on one criteria – it didn't hurt. Remember I was on a whole pain avoiding trip. Omo must have heard me, because she came out and latched on perfectly. I had absolutely no pain.

Now I think the matter was helped by the fact the Piedmont hospital at Rock Hill had an excellent lactation team. They showed me how to get her to latch on.

"Just cup your breast. Wait for her mouth to open wide and just put it in."

It sounds like a simple enough instruction, but it took me quite a few goes to get it. Get it I did, so that was joy incarnate to me. However, the sleepless nights, the constant demands of feeding, the going out and having to sit on public toilets (because very few shops have clocked on they should have breastfeeding chairs for us moms) – all have taken their tolls over the months. Let's not talk about the leaky milk on clothes syndrome. So embarrassing!

When Omo was 6 months and those two little cute teeth up appeared, I thought I would definitely stop feeding her. However, she is now twenty months and has shown no signs of stopping. At first I was anxious for her to stop, but everyone assured me it was healthier for her (she does seem pretty healthy and strong on all that breast milk). In fact, there are many doctors who recommend you go till the baby is two years old.

In my culture many women use to breast feed until the baby was four years old.

Which brings me to some fact sharing. The National Health Information Center reveals "breastfeeding is special for so many reasons." They list the following:

- The joyful bonding with your baby
- The perfect nutrition only you can provide
- The cost savings
- The health benefits for both mother and baby
- In fact, breast milk has disease-fighting antibodies that can help protect infants from several types of illnesses. And mothers who breastfeed have a lower risk of some health problems, including breast cancer and type 2 diabetes.
- Fathers, partners, and other people in the mother's support system can benefit from breastfeeding, too. Not only are there no bottles to prepare, but many people feel warmth, love, and relaxation just from sitting next to a mother and baby during breastfeeding.
- Keep in mind that breastfeeding is a learned skill. It requires patience and practice. For some women, the learning stages can be frustrating and uncomfortable. And some situations make

breastfeeding even harder, such as babies born early or health problems in the mother. The good news is that it will get easier, and support for breastfeeding mothers is growing.

• You are special because you can make the food that is uniquely perfect for your baby. Invest the time in yourself and your baby — for your health and for the bond that will last a lifetime.

In fact they have some excellent breast feeding advice on their website, www.women's health.gov. Many hospitals also have a great lactation team too.

Oh, on a final note about breastfeeding, I have realized However Omo is a clever baby and she seemed to know something we didn't know – all the formula milks are loaded with sugar. I did my research and discovered that sugar in baby formulas in the form of corn syrups etc. can make babies fat, ruin teeth, lead to diabetes and other health problems. In fact this is confirmed in an interesting Parenting.com article entitled Corn Syrup in Formula by a Dr. William Sears who states,

"I share the opinion of many nutritionists and other doctors that the number one cause of the childhood obesity epidemic is the over consumption of HFCS, mainly in the form of beverages."

The Dance of Post Natal Depression

Having support after birthing can be crucial in helping us to adjust to the demands of new motherhood and even fatherhood. For us women the pressure and change of hormones can result in Post Natal depression. Even now many of us are often left to cope alone with this debilitating condition. I still remember how mom supporting me for the first few months after giving birth to Kem Ra helped me so much. This is the traditional Caribbean way.

In many cultures it is believed that the first forty days that follows birthing the mother should be totally supported, and looked after. This makes total sense. In Ayurveda, it is said that the woman should be well looked after for up to 42 days after birth. There is an emphasis on proper lifestyle, nutrition, and thought processes. Throughout this beautiful journey and dance much emphasis has been put on these factors. Keep on putting the Seven Principle of Wellness suggestions into operation. Such as: Meditation, self massage/massage, healthy eating, movement, herbal teas and a positive attitude.

Engaging in proper lifestyle, nutrition and thought leads to good Ojas (that beautiful life giving elixir in the body which boosts immunity, mind-body and soul health). Interestingly, one of the signs of depleted Ojas is low moods. Look back at the Dance of Fertility section for more details on increasing Ojas through the Seven Principles of Wellness.

Sadly there are still many instances where post natal depression is not even acknowledged by ourselves or others. It is worth remembering that if you feel you could be suffering from post natal depression be gentle with yourself, and definitely don't feel ashamed (at least one in seven women suffer from the condition). Here are some of the symptoms of post natal depression. They are very common to ordinary depression:

- Feeling 'low', 'miserable' and tearful for no apparent reason. These feelings persist for most of the time, though they may be worse at certain times of day, particularly the morning.
- Being unable to enjoy yourself. This may be particularly prominent in new mothers who feel that they are not enjoying having a new baby in the way they expected to.
- Irritability is common. This may be with other children, the new baby and particularly with the partner.
- Sleep disturbance is part of looking after a new baby. However in PND there may be additional problems of finding it hard to go to sleep even though you are tired, or waking early in the morning.
- Given that looking after a young baby means having less sleep than usual, it is no surprise that mothers often feel they have no energy. This can be even worse in mothers with PND.
- Appetite is sometimes affected, with mothers not being interested in food. This can be a particular

problem since new mothers need all the energy they can get to look after their babies.

- Anxiety frequently occurs in PND. This may take many forms. It may be feeling tense and 'on edge' all the time. Normal concerns and anxieties that any mother feels for a new baby may become overwhelming. In addition mothers may experience 'panic attacks', which are episodes lasting several minutes when they feel as if something catastrophic is about to happen – such as collapsing, having a heart attack or stroke. These are extremely frightening, but they get better on their own.

- Depression is often accompanied by feelings of being 'worthless' and 'hopeless'. These feelings are common in PND. All mothers are faced with new and sometimes difficult problems with a new baby. However, mothers with PND feel all the more 'not able to cope' and unable to see a way through their difficulties.

- When people are depressed, they sometimes feel that there's no way out of their problems and that they, and their family, would be better off dead. Thoughts of suicide are therefore not uncommon. If you feel this way, it's important that you talk to somebody about how you feel, since there are ways out of your difficulties other than suicide. You should also be aware that your child would be at increased risk of developing mental health problems of their own if you do commit suicide. If you fear that somebody you know feels suicidal, take this seriously and try to talk to them about it. Talking about suicide does

NOT increase the risk of the person committing suicide. Strongly advise the person to visit their doctor.

Besides the things already suggested for post natal depression, one can also take herbal teas and tinctures which aim to balance the mood, and increase our sense of wellbeing. So Chasteberry to balance the hormones could be a good idea, along with St Johns Wort and Avena Sativa tincture (Oats tincture)

Very Balancing Tea

Ingredients
4 tablespoons of Nettles
2 tablespoons of Lemongrass
1 tablespoon of Chasteberry
1 teaspoon of St Johns Wort

Directions
Simmer all ingredients in small pot of water for
fifteen minutes. Strain. Add milk and honey to
taste. Nettle herb is renowned for its restorative,
tonic properties and profuse amounts of iron.
Lemongrass adds a tasty and balancing tone to this
combo. Chasteberry is a hormonal balancer, while
St Johns Wort is a renown natural mood enhancer.

The Dance of Sleepless Nights & Baby Colic

My quest for sleep began to resemble the frantic search for the Holy Grail! Lucky I was not totally unprepared. I had made a Sleep Balm loaded with Chamomile before she was born. This moment of inspiration was triggered by the memory of Kem Ra's constant crying after he was born. Back then I had just started on my wellness path so I really did not know what to do to stop his wailing. Not until he was just over a year old and my mum started an aromatherapy course and discovered the wonder properties of Chamomile to induce calm. It worked. I had a calmer son.

Soon after Omo was born I began to massage her with the chamomile balm. It became mine and Derrick's life saver. That's why I believe every mum should always have Chamomile herb and essential oil in their kitchen cupboard. To find out more about the therapeutic benefits of chamomile just look back over the pregnancy section. Not just chamomile, but massaging the little ones is also of great benefit. Massage helps: you create a good relationship with the baby, the baby to feel safe and loved, to stimulate different body systems (immune system, circulation, digestion), and enhances development.

Although, the Chamomile balm did help Omo to sleep, colic was a real problem that kept us all up at nights. It was like a monster in the closet. Trying to find solutions for it was like trying to find gold dust in desert sand. But the research paid of I discovered that the following truly helped to alleviate Omo's colic:

Warm Castor Oil: This is a traditional Ayurvedic remedy which is renowned for soothing upset Vata conditions such as windy stomachs. Just massage it into the baby's stomach in circular motions.

Acidophilus: Research shows that this friendly bacteria can help cut colic by almost 50%. I found that it helped to cut little Omo's colic by at least 90%. It isn't the cheapest thing on the market to buy. It is however worth its weight in gold as it affords f more restful nights.

Kyro Corn Syrup: This remedy was recommended by my pediatrician. I was wondering how Corn Syrup helps alleviate gas. But it really did help Omo bring up the excess gas she had in her stomach.

Reducing Colicky foods: Yes, there is such a thing as colicky foods. Foods that help produce gas in the baby. They are caffeine, dairy products, citrus fruits, citrus vegetables, cauliflower, cabbage, and spicy foods.

Herbal Teas: Believe it when I drank several cups of freshly brewed chamomile Omo's stomach calmed right down. I also noticed she slept better. Fennel Tea is also good for helping to alleviate colic. Now and again I have put a mild solution of Chamomile tea in Omo's water. The University of Maryland Medical Center also recommend that you can do this. Before you do I would advise you to get the advice of your pediatrician first.

Just a quick note on how to know when your little one is suffering from colic. Some of the signs are:

- Your baby cries for more than 3 hours on at least three occasions a week, but is otherwise healthy.

- Your baby kicks a lot, pulls their legs up close, and makes tight fists.
- Your baby's tummy seems hard, and the baby burps and passes gas often.
- The crying sounds like your baby is in great pain.
- Your baby spits up frequently after feeding.

How long does colic normally last? Most experts say it starts from two weeks and ends at about four months. I found it amusing to read articles that said "Know that the colic will only last for four months". It's obvious those articles were written by individuals who have never had a child with colic. Let's face it. When you do have a colicky baby four months can feel like a hell of a long time. Enough time to end up gibbering nonsense to yourself!

That's why it's so empowering to know there are natural remedies which will help you hold on to your sanity during that colicky period. Also there is nothing pleasant about seeing our little ones in so much pain. Then there's daddy. You really realize that the observation in John Gray's "Men are From Mars and Women Venus" was really true. Men like to find solutions to problems. When they can't they feel frustrated and helpless. That was Derrick. When he could not help with Omo's crying, and when even his "Rock, Rock Wee" (as he called his special trademarked rocking technique) didn't work he was seriously on edge. So he too was glad when we started using remedies that helped to calm her.

Sleep and Colic Reminders

For Peaceful Sleep
Massage with Chamomile Oil

For Colic
Massage baby's stomach with Castor Oil
Give baby Acidophilus
Give baby Kyro Corn Syrup
Cut out colic producing foods from your
diet: caffeine, dairy products, citrus fruits,
citrus vegetables, cauliflower, cabbage, and
spicy foods
Drink Chamomile and Fennel herbal tea

My *Famous* Sleep Baby Oil

Ingredients
1 cup of oil (Soy, Olive, Almond or Sunflower)
1 teaspoon of Vitamin E
Just a few drops of glycerin
10 drops of Chamomile

Directions
Place all ingredients in a bottle. Shake well. Use after bath times to massage baby with. This is also a good oil for a soothing night time massage to help baby sleep.

My Famous Ayurvedic Baby Massage

Get smart and massage that baby. It will make them oh so happy, content, joyful and glowy. Omo is quite spoilt. I massage her every day.

Directions
Make sure room is warm
Baby is covered by a towel (uncover areas to be massaged)
Use gentle rotational touch and flowing strokes
Massage the body in the following sequence:
Legs, feet, hands, chest, stomach, back, face,

The beautiful thing with this massage is that the sequence rules are not set in stone. It is about following your own intuition and baby's preference. Omo hates being on her stomach so her back is always the first place to massage. The important thing with this massage is to maintain its loving flowing strokes.

The Dance of Teething

Omo looks so cute with her first two new teeth, but what a heck of a time she had and we did. Apparently, the vast majority of babies sprout their first teeth when they're between 4 and 7 months of age. They say early starters get their first teeth as early as 3 months. It could be up to a year before a baby gets their first teeth, though.

It's interesting to note that the little sweetie's teeth actually start developing while your baby's in the womb, when tooth buds form in the gums. Teeth break through one at a time over a period of months, and often — but not always — in this order: First the bottom two middle teeth, then the top two middle ones, then the ones along the sides and back. They may not all come in straight, but don't worry — they usually straighten out over time.

Now what about the symptoms of teething. Many experts have varying degrees of advice about it. They are definitely not in unison as to whether teething causes any symptoms at all. If you're a mom though you will know if it does or not. Some experts say that teething causes symptoms like fussiness, swollen gums, drooling, sleeplessness, refusing food, diarrhea, and fever. I agree with them, at least in Omo's case. Cause she had all of those symptoms in huge doses.

The one thing experts agree on is that you should call your child's doctor if your baby has symptoms that worry you or a rectal temperature of 101 degrees F or higher (100.4 degrees F or higher for babies younger than

3 months). The doctor can help determine whether your baby is showing signs of a problem that needs medical attention, like an ear infection. If your baby has loose stools — but not diarrhea — don't worry. The condition will clear up on its own.

We found it quite a challenge finding teething remedies. The things that really worked were the following:

- Teething ring.
- Wash rag in the freezer. When you take it out. Wet the bit the baby will bite on. The cool seems to help alleviate the pain.
- Putting finger in a wash rag and allowing the baby to chew on it.
- Boron's Camilla Teething Relief gel – a homeopathic remedy. Homeopathic remedies appear to be good for teething.
- Keep the face dry to prevent rash from getting worse.

Teething Relief Reminders

These things seem to help:

- Teething ring
- Wash rag in the freezer. When you take it out. Wet the bit the baby will bite on. The cool seems to help alleviate the pain.
- Putting finger in a wash rag and allowing the baby to chew on it
- Boron's Camilla Teething Relief gel – a homeopathic remedy. Homeopathic remedies appear to be good for teething.
- Keep the face dry to prevent rash from getting worse.

The Dance of Eczema

If it's red, scaly and itchy it is most probably baby eczema. Lots of children have eczema during the first year. It shows up on the baby's forehead, cheeks, and scalp, but it can spread to the arms, legs, chest, or other parts of the body. Omo got eczema within the first few months of being born. It was quite distressing seeing it. Her skin was dry, thickened, scaly. She also had tiny bumps. When she scratched her skin it would ooze a little. Apparently, these are all the symptoms of eczema.

Experts say that tendency to eczema is hereditary. I kind of agree, Kem Ra had eczema. I didn't have it as a baby, but I do have very sensitive skin that breaks out even if you look at it too hard. Apparently Eczema can be triggered of by allergens in the baby's food or in the breast milk. The rash can be aggravated by factors like heat, irritants that come in contact with your baby's skin (like wool or the chemicals in some soaps, lotions, and detergents), changes in temperature, and dry skin.

So how do you get rid of the thing? Well, it doesn't seem to be that easy. Even with all my Wellness background I have found it challenging and exhilarating trying to deal with Omo's eczema.

Here are some tips to help:

- First thing the doctors will often recommend is that you keep allergens such as milk out of the baby's diet. Also some babies are allergic to soy milk.

- It is important to keep the baby's skin dry.

- Use hypoallergenic soaps for bathing

- After bath pat don't rub the baby's skin when you are drying them

- Apply a very moisturizing cream. I made a cream for Omo. It has really helped to manage her eczema. One of the key ingredients is Shea Butter, calendula and chamomile herbs. The two herbs mentioned are renown skin calmers

- Don't let baby get too hot

- Avoid itchy materials such as fleeces

- Try and use cotton or organic cotton

- Chose the softest of blankets for the baby to sleep on

- When you go to the doctor they tend to want to give the baby a low dose steroid cream. I did use this for two weeks and it helped to clear up some of the very stubborn scaly skin. My pediatrician did warn that these creams thin out the baby's skin. So should not be used for a long time

- Scratch mitts become a life saver. It stops the little ones from tearing off their skin

- Seeing a herbalist or homeopathic doctor is also a good idea

The good news is that they say children grow out of it.

Eczema Relief Reminders

- First thing the doctors will often recommend is that you keep allergens such as milk out of the baby's diet. Also some babies are allergic to soy milk.

- It is important to keep the babies skin dry.

- Use hypoallergenic soaps for bathing.

- After bath pat don't rub the baby's skin when you are drying them.

- Apply a very moisturizing cream. I made a cream for Omo. It has really helped to manage her eczema. One of the key ingredients is Shea Butter, calendula and chamomile herbs. The two herbs mentioned are renown skin calmers.

- Don't let baby get too hot.

- Avoid itchy materials such as fleeces.

- Try and use cotton or organic cotton.

- Chose the softest of blankets for the baby to sleep on.

- When you go to the doctor they tend to want to give the baby a low dose steroid cream.

- Scratch mitts become a life saver. Seeing a herbalist or homeopathic doctor is also a good idea.

The Dance of Diaper Rash

Omo seemed to have everything else, but diaper rash. God only gives you as much as you can handle! However, recently a client with a five month old baby asked me about how to manage diaper rash naturally. I told her I would do some research. Herbalist David Hoffman quotes a formula from *Natural Child Care* by Maribeth Riggs. Below I quote her directions.

1 Tbl. Chickweed
1 Tbl. Marshmallow Root
1 Tbl. Comfrey Root
1/8 tsp. Golden Seal Root powder
1 cup sweet almond oil
1/4 cup beeswax

1. Combine the Chickweed, Marshmallow Root, Comfrey Root and Goldenseal Root powder in a cast-iron frying pan with the sweet almond oil.
2. Gently fry the mixture for 5 to 10 minutes. Be careful not to let the herbs burn.
3. When the mixture is hot, add the beeswax and melt it down.
4. When the beeswax is completely melted, strain the mixture through a cheese cloth into a small, labeled jar with a tight-fitting lid.
5. Refrigerate the ointment until it solidifies. The final ointment is an opaque tan color and smells of beeswax and Comfrey Root. Keep the ointment in a convenient place near the infant's changing table,

away from heat. Discard any used portion after 2 months.

Application: Apply the ointment by gently rubbing it on the diaper each time the diaper is changed. This ointment is very soothing to a rashy infant. Three or 4 applications are usually enough to get rid of diaper rash. If the infant's diaper rash does not respond to this treatment, or if it keeps reappearing, investigate factors such as the proper disinfection of diapers, changes in diet, or other skin disorders.

David Hoffman suggests that herbs will not usually be enough to clear this problem, unless used in the context of appropriate care being taken with such issues as:

- Change wet diapers promptly and frequently. Switch types of diapers disposable to cloth or reverse.
- Use protective ointment (bees wax, zincoxide, calendula, Diaper Rash Skin Ointment).
- Allow baby to go without diaper, and air and sun dry the area.
- Do not use talcum powder or corn starch. If you must powder, use a clay product.

DANCING THE PATH NOTES

Childbirth is more admirable than conquest, more amazing than self-defense, and as courageous as either one.

Gloria Steinem, Ms. Magazine, April 1981

_____

_____

_____

_____

_____

_____

_____

_____

_____

_____

_____

_____

_____

_____

_____

_____

_____

_____

_____

_____

_____

_____

_____
_____
_____
_____
_____
_____
_____
_____
_____
_____
_____
_____
_____
_____
_____
_____
_____
_____
_____
_____
_____
_____
_____
_____
_____
_____
_____
_____
_____
_____

PART FIVE

THE DANCE OF TRADITION:
Birthing Say Hello to the Past

It was after my beautiful Navajo sister Beth Robertson sent me a power point presentation about Navajo Birthing Rites that I saw many parallels with things my mother had shared with me about Island birthing customs. Even though I have included a few of those things within the pages of this beautiful dance; there were a few I had not. Today I spoke to mom and realized a few things: how important it is to remember the past in order to help create a better future; we often take our own cultural traditions for granted; together we have traditions that are enriching, edifying and spirit nourishing. So to honor the dance of our traditions those from the past, and those we have been creative enough to add - I mention a few birthing conversations I had with some sister friends, including my mom, Remah Joseph.

My Mom - Dancing Birthing the Caribbean Way

Me: Mom you remember you shared with me some things that I had to do when Kem Ra and Omo were born?

Mom: There are so many traditions we have surrounding birth, many of them I can't remember.

Me: What about the one you told me about regarding banding the belly?

Mom: We band the baby's stomach. This is so the navel doesn't grow outward too much. We especially do this with babies who have big belly buttons. We believe that when they cry it pushes the navel out and makes it over protrude. So with these babies we band the stomach. Just lightly, you know. We do it in a way that is comfortable for the baby.

Me: I remember when I had Kem Ra you told me that in the Caribbean they band the woman's stomach.

Mom: I didn't band my own, but yes they do. They wrap a cloth around the woman's stomach. This helps to re-tone the uterus, pull it back in, and to aid in the woman's stomach going down. Now I noticed all the stars are banding their bellies. It has become a fashion, but we have been doing this for a long time.

Me: Is there anything else that is done for the woman after childbirth?

Mom: Yes, we give the woman a castor oil purge to help purify her and ensure that all the afterbirth is out.

Me: Remember how you made me stay in for weeks after giving birth to Kem Ra? I was going crazy. Tell me about that tradition.

Mom: Yes, the woman traditionally has to stay in for weeks. We believe it is easy for pregnant women to catch what we call a cold in the womb. She also needs time to get her energy back.

Me: In terms of the baby I remember you telling us not to cut Kem Ra's hair until he could speak?

Mom: We believe that if you cut the baby's hair before they can talk it causes speech problems. We specially emphasize the boy's hair not being cut because people tend to cut boy's hair more than a girl's.

Me: Yes, I remember how much you fought to make sure we didn't cut his hair before he can talk. There were some more baby rituals I had to do, can you talk some more about them?

Mom: One of the major things when the baby is born is that after their bath we stretch the limbs. We put their hands behind their backs, hang them upside down, lie them flat on the back and massage their legs and body with oil. We do all of this so that the baby can be flexible and healthy.

Me: I mention things to do with the cord and the placenta in this book. Do you have anything to share about what is usually done with these?

Mom: We normally bury the cord in a special place. When I say a special place I mean by a tree, like a coconut tree, that the parents have chosen to plant the cord besides. That tree becomes the child's tree for the rest of their lives.

Me: I know dreams are important to us during pregnancy?

Mom: Yes, as we believe the child is coming in from the spirit world we pay attention to dreams. During pregnancy and even before - you can start receiving dreams about the child. Remember how we both dreamed you were pregnant with a baby boy one year before you became pregnant with Kem Ra?

Me: What about that stuff you told me about putting a tape measure on the door when Kem Ra was having nightmares?

Mom: this is something we do even with adults, but if a child is having nightmares we put a tape measure on the door to keep the negative spirit bothering them occupied. You know they get busy with counting the markings. We also put a red vest on the child to keep away negative spirits. This is done if the child is being bothered by negative energies.

Me: I just remembered something, with each pregnancy I had you made sure I did not have a baby shower. You felt so strongly about this. Can you share with everyone what that's all about?

Mom: We believe that it is bad luck to buy baby clothes before the baby is born. You are suppose to wait.

Me: Remember I thought that there could be a practical explanation behind that. You know in the Caribbean we don't have money to just blow like that!

Mom: Yes, you could be right. It may be practical. You know back in those days there was no ultra sound. So if you buy a whole set of baby girl clothes, and it's a boy what happens then?! But there may be a spiritual dimension. The child in the womb could be the focus of negative energy, so we try to avoid an over focus on the baby until they are born.

Beth - Dancing With Birth the Navajo Way

For the Dine birth is where everything begins. It begins right with conception. As a result the carrying mother (mother to be) has to take very good care of herself and the unborn. The father has to do the same too. After birth, after the child is born into this glittering world his or her pre-natal history is important.

We believe the unborn child is very vulnerable to the outside world. If the parents are careless while the child is still in the womb then the baby will have the imprints of that carelessness. So you have to make sure the Carrying Mother (Mother to be) is careful with what she does. You have to ensure the child is physically and spiritually healthy.

Before the woman gives birth there is a Blessing Way ceremony to ensure the birth goes well. After the woman gives birth there is another Blessing Way ceremony. The woman does not attend either ceremony, someone goes in her place. This is because we believe the birthing mother is very vulnerable during these times to outside energies. The mother can attend the Blessing Ways after the first two. Then eventually the child can take his/her own seat when they can sit up on their own properly.

In the birthing process it is common for the midwives and medicine men to work together. Corn is often sprinkled – this represents life itself. You know without pollen from the plants we wouldn't be here. Everything comes from pollen. It is one of the major chain where our food source begins. We use pollen in all our ceremonies and often put it on our forehead, on top our heads and often touch it to your hearts. You never think of something so small having so much relevance.

The Sash Belt is also an important part of the birthing process. I am not sure where the idea originally came from, but I know it is an inter-tribal thing. It is even used as far as Central and South America. There's a dance that we do with that belt. It is called The Sash Belt Dance.

When we are born it is said the Holy Ones send the winds into us, and it goes all around and settles in our heart where it stays. That wind directs all our movements, and everything about us. Our thumbs and fingers are said to have the whorls of the impressions that are made from those winds. Each finger and its whorls represent a different type of wind.

Once the child is born there is still a big responsibility. We believe that the child has to be spiritually, physically and emotionally nourished. The child is a sacred person. This is why when we had our children forced to Boarding Schools by the Settlers it was agonizing for us. The spirits of those children were not looked after. In fact, many were used for experiments, and bore the scars of those terrible times.

Josie - Dancing With Birth the Heart Way

Here is my birth story as written on the Unassisted Birth forum on Mothering.com two days after Meika was born. I was going to go in and edit and rewrite, but after reading it tonight, I decided that it's perfect. This is what it was like, without any flare. This birth was my second Unassisted Homebirth and my first Unassisted Pregnancy (actually, many people and subtle beings assisted me during both, but UP is the sort of official name for going it without medical advice). My full name is Josephine ("Josie") Edith Furlough Carney Hammond. Before I start my story I just want you all to know some of the following.

I come from a modern working class Southeastern U.S. family. When my mother decided to have a birth without pain medication in the eighties with me, her sisters scoffed at her. Twenty three years later, I had to find my own path in a community where trusting one's own body over the modern allopathic medical industry was still highly ridiculed.

I read piles of books, articles, watched birthing videos, and found a fantastic Unassisted Birth community at Mothering.com. I used some herbs like red raspberry leaf and nettles throughout my pregnancy. The key, though, to my and my daughter's well being was the confidence I found in the center of my being when I tuned out all other voice and listened to my own. Although I had never been taught any helpful traditions by my family (besides my mother's encouragement to follow my heart), I knew that I had in my own body the innate knowledge that transcends any knowledge of the intellect. It is the oldest tradition of all, going back long before the medicine women, long before the words or symbols. It is the true animal tradition of giving birth without hindrance.

My biggest suggestions to any pregnant Mama is to sit in silence for at least five minutes every day and to trust your own insight above all else. You can learn more from the silence than you will from any midwife or doctor. Inform yourself, for information is power. Make the decisions that you believe will be best for you and your baby. Our ability to reason and plan are vital, but remember that your brain is not going to birth this baby. Your body will. She knows how in her own unique way. This is the universal tradition.

The Story

Mamas, I always knew birth could be like this! I feel like over the past three years I've been on a journey and have finally found what I was looking for -- transforming my family, my life and my spirit! It is a journey I will continue to be on throughout the rest of my life and isn't specific to birth. It's about awareness, connection, intuition, and self love and trust.

At the stroke of midnight, 7 February 2008, I woke up to pee. As soon as I stood up, a trickle went down my leg. "Am I peeing on myself?" I thought -- at this point, it was completely plausible! my water had broken with both my other two right before pushing in a big gush, so

I had no experience with the "trickly waters" phenomenon. After going to the restroom and walking around for a little while, though, I decided that I couldn't possibly be THAT incontinent even with my little one riding low on my bladder. Still, I thought, labor could be hours away. I'd been stuck in prodromal labor land for a week or more and didn't want to get my hopes up. So I decided to clean the bathtub, fix myself some tea and take a nice bath. If something's going to happen in the bath, I thought, I'll know it's the real thing.

By the time I decided it was going to happen that night, it had been about 1.5hr since my water started dribbling. I woke my husband, David, up and he came and hung out with me in the bath for a little while through two or three contractions. He said, "do you think we should call mom?" [To come get our 18month old, Kai] I almost said no, let's wait, but then a contraction came that made me pay attention. "

Okay," I said, "I guess I'd really like to just pay attention to these. I'm really jealous of those women who can have their toddlers with them -- but I think it'll be too distracting for me." So at 2am, David called his mom and she came over to get Kai. By the time they had left, I was still walking around, stopping for contractions and telling David and his mom not to talk to me.

Then they left, I went into the bedroom. I told David that I'd like to be by myself for a little while. He had already set up candles and music and burnt some sage in the bedroom -- it was a perfect, quiet, safe little den. I told him the only thing I was worried about was anyone invading my space. I asked him to keep guard (we lived in a big house with his father, grandmother and grandfather. I wanted to make sure that if I woke anyone, they'd know to stay out of our side of the house). He had no problem with this and assured me that he was there to do whatever I needed.

In the bedroom, I felt the need to empty myself out. I had a five gallon bucket and whenever I'd have a contraction, I could feel that I had to make a bowel movement (TMI, I know -- but, hey, that's birth!). During some contractions I had to bare down, during some I didn't. The ones that I didn't, I walked around the room, swinging my legs back and forth, or held onto the dresser and bent over at the waste. Whatever it was, I had to keep moving the whole time. If I stopped, it hurt.

If I danced, it was powerful! At some point, I knew I was done emptying out and called David in to take my bucket outside to get the smell out (oh my god, this is love, right?!). I was starting to feel tired and was resting on the futon in between contractions. I told David "I'd like you in here, but you're still distracting me." then I put on my sleep mask thingy (like a blindfold) -- so that I couldn't concentrate on David, even if I wanted to.

After a couple of minutes, he had successfully turned himself into a tiny fly on the wall and wasn't bothering me at all. I don't know how he did this, but he managed to shift his energy so that I could focus. At this point, I wasn't getting up for the contractions any more, but was staying on my hands and knees I also had started making noises through them. Low, moaning noises that started in my gut and, as they came up, became the roar of a screaming train. Right around this point, the thought ran through my head, I should have gone to the hospital so they could give me drugs!. I said to David with a little smirk, "I think I'm in transition."

I was getting pretty tired at this point. i wanted to be on my hands and knees, but my arms were shaking. so I moved over to the dresser and put one of the big hospital grade pads we have under me. That way, I could hold on to the dresser while on my knees. after one or two contractions that way, I could feel that my body was about to push. "OOoooohhhh that feels SO GOOD!!" at this point my head was under the dresser (there's like a 2x3 cubby space there) and I was just riding the contractions, letting them push when they came and just feeling it.

At one point the thought came into my head "I never want to do this again" then, immediately, the next thought: "I might NEVER do this again!" I'd better pay attention!! Very soon i reached down and felt her beautiful little face. I must have backed up somewhat then because David's hand accidentally touched my back side and I screamed "DONT TOUCH ME!" poor David .. The next push brought Meika into my arms -- open eyed, pink and crying. As soon as I got a towel around her she settled down. She sneezed a few times to get out some snot bubbles. David said she looked like Gollum from lord of the rings. It was true. David's dad was in the other room and said that he heard her cry at exactly 3am.

I can't even describe how perfect this birth and the time since then has been. I have so much more faith in myself -- but not myself. I mean, I have faith in everything, and I have faith in my place in everything. I know that I don't have to DO anything to make it happen. Ah. I'm ranting. Two days later, I'm still high on endorphins from my little wonder.

Thank you all for your support and knowledge, and mostly for your faith in the universe and in women and babies and life

Derrick – The Male Dancing With Birth

My heart goes out to the Great Mother, and all those mothers that hold and reflect her strength, compassion, and unconditional Love. When contemplating the difference between the female and male genders throughout the various species, I have resolved that it is the female that is truly endowed with the sacred powers required to successfully perpetuate and nurture life on Earth. This is no small matter. Each life is sacred, and part of the whole, the Universe. It is the Universe that decides to allow a new life to form and then to be born in a particular location in the cosmos, at a specified time, and to a pair of designated caretakers. We (humans) take this event way too lightly don't we?

Well, the Mother IS a special breed. I no longer can pretend to be the head of the house. I bow down to the awesomeness of Motherhood. Of course, that includes way more than one can fit into a book, and not come even close to it in a preamble. None the less, hear me out; I must say just a little something to this Mother, the Great Mother, and all the Mothers in this vast Universe of ours from my heart.

I have borne witness of the sacred act of conception. This is what comes after sacred contemplation of the child that a loving pair wishes to bring into their existence. Once we consider the circumstances of the day and place in which we live, the impact of our ancestors upon us and the world, and even the potential that that child may (or may not) have on this place / the world / the Universe; we smile and confirm that we definitely do want to project this energy that we share between us.

I have borne witness to the sacred womb. This is the first world that this precious cargo begins their journey into our time and space. We cannot actually reach out and touch, but we know the child is real, alive, and sacred right away. I remember the first heartbeat and kick and wiggle. And the womb surely should be safe, peaceful, stable, pure, loved, well fed, and showered with the loving voices and the presence of the new family at all times.

I have borne witness to the sacred birth. All births are extraordinary, I witnessed my daughters Shanté and Kanika Lewis' births and Wow! But this one was EXTRAordinary, it was at home into my hands, an unplanned – superbly executed home birth. Thanks to Omileye and her wellness body and ways. Let's face it my fellow male species, we would not want to nor could we even ever give birth through any part of our body. In fact, it is a huge challenge to actually survive just witnessing this miracle.

And by no means, is waking up hundreds of times over the coming months, breastfeeding, burping, soothing, cuddling, rocking, changing, cleaning... a walk in anyone's park! Anytime I get to thinking that I got the short end of the stick because I have to work and Omi gets to stay home with this lovely being that greets me with love and joy when I come home; I get hit right between the eyes, when Mom has to take a day off, rare but oh so real, and I get a full dose of the little miracle's day long routine, OMG! It definitely takes a mother's love. Much respect!

So to all you Mothers out there – I sincerely apologize! I apologize for allowing any of you to be treated less than the goddesses that you truly are. It is my sincere prayer that all males will elevate you from this day forward and help to create the right universe for our lovely sacred future as one. I Shall.

About the Author

Omileye Achikeobi –Lewis is hails from the UK and is of Caribbean origin. She is a Journalist, author, fifth generation healer, Master Energy Healer, Ayurvedic Practitioner. She is absolutely passionate about helping others to dance the dance of joy in every aspect of their lives. She lives in South Carolina, with her husband, and two children: Kem Ra and Omololu.

She conducts numerous life healing workshops. She we also be conducting Birthing workshop and life healing workshops in collaboration with Beth Robertson, Navajo Master Weaver of wool and life, and other women who hold the same vision of helping women and indidividuals awaken to the power of birthing in every stage of life and life.

Contact Omileye at www.yeyeosun.com
YeyeOsun, The Institute of Energy Medicine and Life Leadership

Other Books by Author

Also by Omileye Achikeobi-Lewis
(aka Ezolaagbo Achikeobi):
A Journey Through Breath
I Pray for Healing
Seven Principles of Wellness
In The Spirit of Wellness
Dreamtime Awakening
Beautiful Waters
see also:
Yeye Osun at www.yeyeosun.com

About Lori Portka, Her Art and the Front Cover of "Ploop!"

Lori's art has a natural way of inspiring something magical from the depths and creative womb of others. Her picture, "Lift Her Up to the Sky" used for the front cover deeply moved and inspired author Omileye in the final touches of "Ploop! the Abundant Pregnancy Journey"

You can view more of Lori's beautiful art at www. loriportka.com

Bibliography

Achikeobi-Lewis, Ezolaagbo. Dreamtime Awakening. Naked Truth Press, 2009.

Achikeobi, Ezolaagbo. A Journey Through Breath. X Press, 1996/

Achikeobi, Ezolaagbo. I Pray for Healing. Naked Truth, 2009.

Achikeobi-Lewis, Omileye.Ezolaagbo. Seven Principles of Wellness. Naked Truth Press, 2010

Achikeobi-Lewis. Omileye.Ezolaagbo. In The Spirit of Wellness, Naked Truth Press, 2010

Aiken, Bill. Seven Sacred Rivers. Penguin Books, 1992.

Barocovcin, Helen. The Way of a Pilgrim. Doubleday, 1997.

Bennett, Hal and Mike, Samuels. The Well Body Book. Random House, 1973.

Bennett, Zina and Sparrow Susans. Follow Your Bliss. Avon Books, 1990.

Bly, Robert. A Little Book on the Human Shadow. Harper San Francisco, 1988.

Bohm, David. 1957. Causality and Chance in Modern Physics, 1961 Harper edition reprinted in 1980 by Philadelphia: U of Pennsylvania Press

Butree, M Julia. The Rhythm of the Redman: In Song, Dance and Decoration. A.S Barnes, 1930.

Cleary, Thomas and Sartaz, Aziz. Twilight Goddess: Spritual Feminism and Feminine Spirituality. Shambala, 2002.

Coleman, Daniel, Ecological Intelligence. Broadway Books, 2009.

Cousins, Norman. The Healing Heart. Avon. Books, 1984.

Cross, John. Acupuncture and Chakra Energy System. North Atlantic Books, 2008.

Frankhauser Jerry. The Power of Affirmations. Coleman Graphics, 1983.

Gandhi, Mahatma. Peace. Blue Mountain Arts. Inc.,2001.

Gennep, Arnold. The Rites of Passage. University of Chicago Press, 1960.

Ghanaian Festivals:www.gsu.edu/afinijws/emmal/html

Gray, Martin. Sacred Earth. Sterling Publishing, 2007.

Hall, Judy. The Encyclopedia of Crystals. Octopus Publishing, 2006.

Hoffman, David. Medical Herbalism. Inner Traditions Bear & Company, 2003.

Holika: www.indiaexpress.com/rangolia/holi/html

Jung, Carl. Man and His Symbols. Dells, 1968.

Jung, CJ. The Structure and Dynamics of the Psyche. RFC. Hull, Vol 8 by Collected Works. Princeton University Press, 1960.

Komfield, Jack. The Path with Heart. Bantam, 1993.

Lama, Dalai Lama. The Dalai Lama's Book of Love and Compassion. Thorsons, 2002.

Leshan, Lawrence. How to Meditate. Boston: Little Brown, 1974.

Lewis, C.S. Miracles. Macmillian, 1947.

Lidell, Lucy. The Sivananda Companion to Yoga. Fireside Book, Simon & Schuster, inc., 1983.

Lilly, Sue and Lilly Simon. Healing with Crystals & Chakra Energies. Annes Publishing Ltd, 2003.

Locke, Steven and Douglas, Collison. The Healer Within. Dutton, 1986.

LockHart, R.A. "Cancer in Myth and Dream". An Annual of Archetypal Psychology and Jungian Thought, 1977: 1-26.

Loy Krathong Festival: www.geocites.com/siamsmile 365/loigratongl/html

Marchant, Kerena, Sloan Frank, Gryspeeroff Rebecca. The Book of Hindu Festivals. Raintree, 2001.

Mckay, Alex. The History of Tibet. Routledge, 2005.

Mindell, A. Working with the Dreaming Body. Routledge & Kegan Paul, 1985.

Moore, Thomas. Care of the Soul. Haper Perennial, 1992.

Moorey, Teresa. Secrets of Moon Astrology. A Godsfield Book, 2006.

Murkoff, Heidi. What to Expect When You are Expecting. Workman Publishing, 2008.

Olson, Carl. The Book of the Goddess Past and Present. Crossroad, 1986.

Oyle, Irving. The Healing Mind. Pocket Books, 1975.

Peck, Scott. The Road Less Traveled. Simon & Schuster, 1978.

Patricia Davis, Aromatherapy an A-Z, Daniel, 1999

Pierre, Mark and Long Soldier, Tilda. Walking in The Sacred Manner. Touchstone, 1995.

Pollard III, John. Self Parenting. Generic Human Studies Publishing, 1987.

Post, Laurens. The Lost World of The Kalahari. William Morrow, 1958.

Ravern, Hazel. Crystal Healing. Raven & Co Publishing, 2000.

Robinson, Jonathan. Shortcuts to Bliss. Conari Press, 1998.

Rocks and Minerals. Parragon, 2008.

Roman, Sanaya and Duane Packer. Creating Money. H.J. Kramer, 1988.

Siegal, Bernies. Peace, Love & Healing. Haper & Row Publishers, 1989.

Simon, Sidney. Setting Unstuck: Breaking Through Barriers of change. Warner Books, 1988.

Some Patrice, Malidoma. Off Water and The Spirit, Penguin. 1995.

Starhawk. The Spiral Dance. Harper and Rows, 1997.

Stovall, Jim. The Ultimate Shift. River Oak, 2001.

Struthers, Jane. Working with Aura. Godsfield Press, 2006.

Sumiyoshi, S, ed.Nigerian Culture and Customs: A Walk Through Time. Koemar, 1996.

Suzuki, David and MC Connell, Amanda. The Sacred Balance. Greystone Books, 2002.

Tzu, Lao. Tao Te Ching. Penguin, 1963.

Walsh, Roger. The Spirit of Shamanism. J.P Tancher, 1990.

Whitfield Charles. Healing The Inner Child Within. Health Communications, 1987 Iyengar, BKS.

B.K.S. Light on Life. Rodale, 2008

I embrace my inner wisdom

www.ingramcontent.com/pod-product-compliance
Lightning Source LLC
LaVergne TN
LVHW011220080426
835509LV00005B/224